OUT OF TIME

OUT OF TIME;

History and Evolution in Anthropological Discourse. Second Edition

Includes New Afterword

NICHOLAS THOMAS

Ann Arbor
THE UNIVERSITY OF MICHIGAN PRESS

A CIP catalog record for this book is available from the British Library.

Thomas, Nicholas, 1928–
    Out of time : history and evolution in anthropological discourse /
Nicholas Thomas. — 2nd ed., includes new afterword.
      p.   cm.
    Includes bibliographical references and index.
    ISBN 0-472-08377-5 (pbk.)
    1. Ethnology—Philosophy. 2. History. 3. Social evolution.
4. Ethnology—Polynesia. 5. Polynesia—History. I. Title.
GN345.2.T48 1996
306′.01—dc20   96-13807
                                        CIP

for Margaret Jolly

I feel the earth move under my feet.
I feel the tumbling down tumbling down

Einstein on the beach (1976)

Contents

Acknowledgements

Although this book was mostly written in Cambridge in the first half of 1987, the ideas put forward in it developed over a longer period. My debts to colleagues, students, friends and other writers are as numerous as the conversations and bits of reading which had even a tangential bearing on the questions discussed here. For their advice and comments on drafts I am grateful in particular to Pascal Boyer, John Dunn, Johannes Fabian, Anthony Giddens, Chris Gregory, Caroline Humphrey, Roger Keesing and Tanya Luhrmann; for teaching me a lot about Pacific history I thank Niel Gunson; I am grateful also to King's College for providing an environment which enabled me to write the book. I owe more than I can say to Margaret Jolly's encouragement and intellectual help. Special thanks also to Anna Jolly, who helped keep me going.

Introduction

Anthropologists and other social scientists have often attempted to resolve the split between the historical study of change over time and a sociological or anthropological analysis of systems at a particular time – which often in fact takes them out of all time. Although it is widely recognized that there is something fundamentally wrong with an ahistorical social science – just as there is with a history which neglects the structural properties of social and cultural phenomena – these efforts have only recently borne much fruit. Anthropologists have attempted to include history, or even started to write history, and historians have drawn on particular sociological or anthropological concepts. The broader impact of these tendencies is not yet apparent: from some perspectives, central concerns have been transformed; others display what a recent reviewer of Roy Wagner has dubbed 'a considered disregard for revived anthropological interests in (conventional) history and practice' (Foster 1987: 155). It might be asserted that much recent anthropological history has delighted in the unconventional, but the point is precisely that this is not acknowledged – that a separation might be maintained between a distinct 'historical' endeavour and whatever anthropology is. There is certainly no unified theory of cultural or social systems in history. However, because modern life involves both so much change and such manifestly pervasive systems as, for instance, the world economy, attempts to integrate these kinds of knowledge might even be taken to be central to a better knowledge of our contemporary situation.

The surge of interest in the history/anthropology conjuncture has seen relatively little sustained discussion of precisely why anthropology was, and to some extent continues to be, ahistorical. This book is about what it means for anthropological texts and comparative discussions to be 'out of time'. Failure to address this question can only lead to an implicit perpetuation of the flaws of earlier work. It is apparent that history is often introduced in order to deny its significance. History has not been neglected simply through an oversight, but for complex conceptual and discursive reasons. Only an analysis of the conditions of anthropological writing which set the discourse out of time can enable us to transcend these constraints.

In attempting to depict, criticize and transcend the conventions and representations of a discipline 'out of time', I resort in what follows to a polemical collage – polemical in the sense that it demands reconstruction rather than mere revision in the social sciences (and anthropology in particular); and a collage in the sense that its claims are worked out through several different registers. I have jumbled together epistemological critique, evolutionary theory, substantive revision of Polynesian anthropology, and some discussion of the history of anthropological ideas about the Pacific. With respect to the last, I do not contribute to a history of ideas for itself, but simply present certain stories which are subordinated to the objectives of my critique.

In case it is thought that this jumble arises simply from a playful desire to destabilize reigning categories, I should emphasize that these typically distinct discourses are brought together precisely because one of the main lines of my argument is that they are implicitly tangled to a much greater degree than is normally acknowledged. My demonstration aims not simply to prove this, but to establish that it matters. I draw upon the cases of historical and evolutionary ideas; the former the subject of much current discussion in anthropology, the latter occupying, I argue, a crucial but undisclosed position in the logic of the discipline. I offer reformulations of approaches to both evolution and history, and in this context the epistemological discussion assumes a different significance: it becomes less a general argument to be exemplified, and more a set of issues internal to the more specific problem of reshaping certain anthropological constructs – which, to complete the circle, is another way of asserting the degree of entanglement mentioned above. The project is neither strictly epistemological nor purely analytical: the aim is rather to demonstrate, through discussion of anthropological discourse on Polynesia, that the development of a more satisfactory perspective cannot take place without a pattern of theoretical and interpretive shifts in apparently distinct realms. The value of one apparently specific or purely theoretical critique or revision may thus arise less from its direct implications than from what it produces in another context.

An initial distinction between what I have done and much other recent anthropological writing on epistemology and the general orientation of the discipline may be helpful. This arises from the emphasis in general on what amounts to a subjective angle, on the ethnographer's knowing and knowledge. It is as though all the problems are tied up with experience and procedures in the field, and with the constructs which the so-called 'writing-up' of fieldwork generates (e.g. Clifford and Marcus 1986; Marcus and Fischer 1986; Borofsky 1987). This dimension is certainly important, and I too would want to emphasize that 'academic and literary genres in-terpenetrate' (Clifford 1986: 2), but my concern is mainly with the reading rather than the making of anthropological texts, with the discourses of anthropological genres and theories, of both ethnography and interpretation, rather than reflection upon the formation of the units of ethnographic knowledge. Anthropology is not just ethnography; in fact, the meanings which can be attached to ethnographic case studies depend on wider schemes, on classifications of societies, and on polemics which generate interest in particular projects at particular times. Anthropological works are moreover constantly drawn into comparative studies, syntheses, and re-analyses within the discipline, as well as purposes on the margins such as the contextualization of museum objects, and a variety of more definitely 'popular' uses. At this level the texts must be seen as a set of cultural products; the individual ethnographer's knowledge ceases to be the appropriate frame for critical discussion.

Two statements about what this book is not: first, it avoids case studies which illustrate in any extensive way the proposed approach to evolution and history. The discussions of Pacific material are merely illustrative (although they draw partly on more extensive treatments published elsewhere). A reader who feels that nothing short of an extended case study can be persuasive will, of course, remain unpersuaded, but the extent of my discussion of Polynesian histories is only proportionate with the need to work through an example from a number of distinct angles. Secondly, I do not deal with questions specifically about historical knowledge, or the constitution of 'ethnohistory' as a subdiscipline, such as the relation between indigenous views of history and the historical constructions of European scholars. These are of considerable importance in parts of the Pacific and Africa, among other places, but would require an extensive discussion of the politics of knowledge in particular regions, and are only contingently related to the more general issues I pursue here. I would want, in any case to avoid the notion that the subject-matter of this work is 'ethnohistory', that is, a marginal overlap between history and anthropology, which might be developed in certain ways which have no particular implications for either core discipline. My aim, and what I take to be the aim of a number of other writers, is a more consequential conjuncture of history and anthropology, which transforms, rather than merely links, each of the two practices; as Cohn has observed, one seeks to create 'not just...another new specialty, not just...the means by which more hyphenated histories and anthropologies may be generated, but...the means by which an epistemology and a subject matter common to the two disciplines might be reasserted' (1980: 216).

I have refrained from extended definitional discussion of terms such as 'evolution' and 'history', because I take the view that meanings subsist in the uses of concepts in texts, rather than in authorial pronouncements which may bear little relation to the order of a discourse. There is, of course, a tension between former characterizations – in which history is an empirical

3

succession of events and evolution refers to progressive development – and a merging of meanings in a more satisfactory analysis of change which is processual and systemic but neither directed nor abstracted. There are thus certain shifts in the implicit definitions manipulated here, and presumably the point of theoretical argument is an alteration of meanings of concepts. I do not attempt to further complicate this work by engaging in some kind of auto-analysis of the book's 'writing up'. However, I may forestall some criticism by pointing out that I use history to mean events and social processes rather than the knowledge of such events and processes. Cultural and epistemological issues about traditions, and the representation of events and actions must be dealt with, but entail problems which are quite distinct from the substantive and theoretical questions of historical effect, with which I am more concerned here.[1]

This distinction may be meaningless to those who take the view that past events have no bearing on a social situation or cultural order unless they are perceived and imagined by the actors involved, unless they are part of what is recognized as a salient 'history'. The theoretical step of equating all history with history as it is perceived can be seen as a reaction to an intransigent, positivist account which insists that socially objective history is a process of real past events which can only be more or less imperfectly mirrored in historical narrative. The positivist view neglected the fact that histories are produced, that particular depictions employ cultural codes, carry political agendas, and impose various kinds of narrative metaphors – they are, in short, anything but 'faithful' or unproblematic representations. Noticing that histories are written, and repudiating the positivists' preoccupation with an exhaustive (and therefore inaccessible) image of the past, should not, however, lead us to scrutinize nothing other than historical representations, or insist that there is no reality external to such representations. The distinctiveness of particular social self-images frequently arises from the circumstances which they express and mediate, and the origins and determinants of particular ways of seeing often lie beyond, or are erased by, those visions themselves. Reference must therefore be made to events which are not necessarily taken seriously by the people being considered. This is to expose their world view to question, but if we do not believe that our own national ideologies and cultures should be uncritically sustained, it seems peculiar that other people's representations should be privileged.

In focussing on theoretical aspects of the anthropology–history relationship, I am not, of course, dealing with newly exposed ground. The larger problems of the relation between various kinds of models of social or cultural systems, and temporal processes, have surfaced often enough in the history of social theory, and Giddens (1979, 1981), for example, has recently emphasized the importance of situating practices and social relations in both existential and longer-term time.

Institutions are practices which 'stretch' over long time–space distances in the reproduction of social systems. The structural practices of social systems 'bind' the temporality of the *durée* of the day-to-day life-world to the *longue durée* of institutions, interpolated in the finite span of existence of the individual human being.

(1981: 28)

A parallel, though more specific, theoretical emphasis might be seen in the opening sections of Bourdieu's influential tract on theorizing practice, which exposed the atemporal character of structuralist perspectives on gift exchange (1977: 3–7). The point that temporality should be seen to be constitutive of, rather than marginal to, social and cultural systems is thus well established at a general level, but there has been surprisingly little discussion of what kind of time should become important in social analysis, and surprisingly little consideration of what distinct kinds of intellectual practice a more integrated endeavour would depend upon (but cf. B. Cohn 1980: 220–1). Giddens was concerned primarily with transformations at a general level in the temporal (and spatial) constitution of particular social forms; he emphasized, for instance, that capitalism was predicated on the separation of time as a commoditized, abstract dimension from time as the substance of lived experience (1981: 130–1). This underlines the cultural specificity of the opposition between existence as a condition and an external flow of events, but analysis at the level of social theory does not enable one to reveal the historical constitution of particular social forms or statements. This is, of course, hardly the purpose of social theory, but the consequence is that one must explore analytic procedures at a different level, if one is to effectively incorporate in case studies the implications of theoretical propositions such as Giddens'. Much of the critique of functionalism, structuralism and certain other paradigms has been concerned with the atemporal aspect of those approaches, and the ambiguous or marginal status of time is alluded to at various points in the critiques I develop. My main concern, though, is more specific: it is with the absence of historical time, and with the explicit or implicit negation of the notion that history has any constitutive effect in the social situation under consideration. It is possible for marginal reference to be made to history or the 'historical context' (as in Wagner's [1986] study of the Barok of New Ireland), or for analysis to deal partly with temporal processes (e.g. Munn 1986), without there being any interest in the significance of historical processes in the system being examined.

Various schools of historians, perhaps most notably the Annales group, have been oriented towards 'sociological' history of one sort or another, and historians such as Keith Thomas (1971) and Norman Cohn (1970) have frequently made reference to anthropological insights into such phenomena as witchcraft and millennial movements. It must, however, be recognized that such borrowings, like those which characterized debates about rationality in philosophy and anthropology, did not represent any serious

5

integration of methods or theories. Particular historical problems might have been illuminated, and ethnographies of past societies might have been valuable in their own terms, but an essential separation persisted between analytic narratives of change and development, and systemic expositions to which change was peripheral.

Well-known essays which dwelt upon the negative aspects of the exclusion of history from anthropology were published by such influential anthropologists as Evans-Pritchard (1962)[2] and Lévi-Strauss (1968) many years ago, and these led to some debate, mainly within British social anthropology (e.g. Lewis (ed.) 1968) (since 'history' of a diffusionist sort had never been excluded in American anthropology with quite the same vigour). But what is notable about the discipline is that these critiques had very little effect upon the *core* of anthropological discussion – which has continued to be occupied by the analysis of ethnography, that is, by the systematic but non-historical exploration of problems of ritual, economics, kinship, politics and so on (which is not to say that certain valuable historical anthropological studies have not been produced, but rather that they would not have been identified as canonical anthropological works). In the case of Lévi-Strauss's essay, it is arguable that the admirable views put forward found no expression even in his own major works. This itself suggests that there are more fundamental problems which these authors neglected.

The discipline is permeable, and overlaps with such diverse subjects as geography, aesthetics, archaeology, philosophy and history, and there has thus been a spectrum of 'ethnohistories', works of historical anthropology, and historical studies influenced by anthropological theory. There is a great deal of work which seems to be animated by the conjunction of history and anthropology, but much of this does not transcend the limitations of earlier, ahistorical paradigms. Some studies simply draw evidence from a historical period into a synchronic analysis of a cultural or social system. What is abstracted from time is thus a set of archival sources, rather than a set of fieldwork observations (e.g. Evans-Pritchard 1949; Valeri 1985; cf. Bloch 1987; Geertz 1980). Some other works add much to our knowledge of indigenous perceptions of history or tradition, but do not historicize the indigenous perceptions themselves: the overarching context, and reference point for interpretation, remains an intransigently atemporal culture, rather than a historical process (e.g. Borofsky 1987; Parmentier 1987). The historical context is often mentioned in an introductory or marginal way, but has no genuine analytic role or discursive place (cf. Thomas n.d.2). There have been studies, however, which offer more profound reconstructions of culture in history, and which actually situate their objects of discussion as outcomes of historical processes. Gewertz's study of gender, trading relationships, and the development of hierarchy in a Sepik regional system (1983) provides a good example, as does Moore's analysis of the evolution

6

of Chagga 'customary' law (1986). Comaroff's study, *Body of power, spirit of resistance* (1985), which deals with the development of Barolong (South African) cosmology and ritual in the nineteenth and twentieth centuries, overcomes the anthropological tendency to lapse into talk *either* of power and inequality *or* of meaning and symbolism in its depiction of resistant symbolic practice and anti-colonial culture. Since my concerns are with the incorporation of colonial history in particular, as well as temporal processes in general, in anthropological thought, Comaroff's approach is close to that enunciated here (see also Bloch 1986; Baré 1987; Fabian 1986; Fox 1977; Frankel 1986; Humphrey 1982; Rosaldo 1980; Wood 1982). Other works might be cited, but my point is simply that the exercise undertaken here does not derive from a vacuum, but from a wave of interest in the disciplines of anthropology and history – which in some cases has deeper roots in our desire to connect the sophistication of analysis with the actualities of political and economic crises, and in the mutual entanglement of 'observers' and 'observed' in colonial (or ostensibly 'post-colonial') inequalities.

I am not, however, concerned simply to articulate the premises of recent works in historical anthropology. Many of these are, in any case, concerned much more with local substantive issues than with the question of the compatability or otherwise of particular forms of knowledge. I aim rather to establish what deeper features of anthropological practice and style have made such a conjunction so elusive. As was stated above, this point turns upon a reconsideration of ideas about 'theory' and general epistemological models, and some more specific issues, such as the status of archival sources in anthropology. Since an evolutionary model of some explicit or covert variety has generally taken the place of 'history' as anthropology's chronological frame, a reinstallation of history depends more directly upon a reconstruction of evolutionary notions than most current writing can acknowledge.

Anthropology is a diverse and uneven subject. Arguments which are heretical or contentious for some schools or perspectives are almost axiomatic for others; further elaboration of some points in this work might thus have been desirable for some readers, but tedious for others. It is clear, however, that there is by no means a consensus that anthropological studies of non-western societies should focus upon the colonial entanglement, and the way that this has constituted symbolic orders as well as social and economic relations. Such a view may not be frequently criticized by proponents of other sets of concerns, but the fact that numerous symbolic anthropologists persist in analysing domains of meaning and metaphor without reference to historic context reveals that a theoretical and ideological struggle is taking place – perhaps at the level of personal debate and seminar argument more often than in print. This book aims to synthesize one side of such a debate, though without suggesting that symbolic anthropology is an

7

unprofitable endeavour. Indeed, another angle of my argument, as I have stated, is that some of the theoretical complexities are confounded by anthropological metaphors, which is a way of saying that the discipline and discourse of anthropology itself needs to be analysed symbolically. My claim is not to present an original approach; the argument is rather that if several emerging positions – a kind of cultural critique, a kind of socio-historical analysis, a consciousness of the history (and prehistory) of anthropological writing – are brought together, then another way of seeing the subject can be consolidated. This way is not simply more consistent and inclusive intellectually, but also brings our conceptual efforts into a closer relation with the social experiences and struggles which surround us.

1

History and anthropological discourse

Varieties of anthropology suppose distinct objects of knowledge. The 'customs', savage throught-processes and ideas about magic which preoccupied early ethnologists occupied a different space to social organization and the quasi-organic cultural system of functionalism. There is no less a gap between the ecological processes of cultural materialism and the metaphors and elisions of symbolic analysis. It cannot be suggested that there is some definite thing like 'human culture' containing puzzles which have simply been tackled in different ways by diverse anthropological schools. The thing talked about and the kinds of puzzle that matter are and have been generated by intellectual and political concerns. An emergent set of interests will redefine the object and dismiss some old puzzles. Debates are abandoned more often than resolved. Those who initiate revisions or more radical conceptual departures presumably believe that these will lead to fuller or more relevant explanations and interpretations, depending upon their concerns; toward science or a better understanding, if their bias is positivist or relativist.

The marginalization of history

What follows is in part an argument for such a reorientation. There are great divergences between perspectives in social theory of the kind noted above, but almost all have made objects for attention which are detached from time, and particularly so from the grimy historical time of events and intrusions. In a great many cases temporal and historical processes were simply undiscussed or excluded; where they were not, time and change were understood to be secondary to some field of relationships or entity which was best understood in non-temporal, systemic terms. The view developed here is that historical processes and their effects are internal to social systems and that attempts to analyse societies without reference to history are likely to embody both theoretical errors and substantive misinterpretations. The misrecognition of consequences of colonial penetration as elements of a timeless 'culture' exemplifies most directly the link between specific empirical

9

questions and the deeper blindness of anthropological reasoning, but represents only one sort of effect that the combination of ahistorical theory and good or bad evidence may have in anthropological writing.

The critique cannot be reduced to a 'correction' of misrecognition, of the failure to distinguish recent effects or disentangle invented tradition: 'we simply regarded gender relations and residence patterns among the X as elements of their culture, but now we know that these reflected adaptations to the colonial situation'. Historical appreciations do demand revised understandings but also raise fundamental issues about the nature of the standard objects for anthropological discussion, as well as the research and writing practice which keeps these studied things in intellectual circulation. So long as ethnographic fieldwork is mandatory and historical work marginal in an anthropological career, attempts to alter understanding are doomed to the extent that conceptions of objects arise from the way they are known. There is clearly no absolute determinism in this relationship, but if the discipline continues to give intricate and intimate knowledge of localities a privileged status, one could no more expect anthropologists to appreciate history, than one could expect those who study ancient inscriptions to focus on sentiments in personal interaction. This is partly because ethnography is likely to have a limited bearing on certain issues (such as longer-term change), but also because the elevation of personal ethnographic understanding as the basis for satisfactory description and some mysterious intuitive understanding disables other forms of evidence.[1]

It may be inferred from this that I am not merely concerned to assert that time, and specifically history, is 'more important' than has generally been acknowledged. This has been said often enough, although the core of anthropological practice has not changed as a result.[2] The problem is that 'a historical perspective' cannot simply be added to anthropology as it is. I argue that this would reproduce the fundamental opposition between the 'society' (or 'culture') as the primary thing known, and some subsequent sequence of events, which somehow is not directly linked with the inner properties of the system considered. The discipline's object is a system or structure which has an ordered character precisely because contingency and temporality are excluded. The opposition was developed in the strongest and most self-conscious way by Lévi-Strauss (1966: 233f.) but has a much deeper basis in the history of the human sciences, and could be seen as one of the elementary features of anthropological discourse. The separation is manifested at the larger level in the gap between a kind of narrative history which is now rather old-fashioned, and subjects such as anthropology and sociology, and also in the foundation of modern anthropology at the moment of the exclusion of diachronic diffusionism (or evolutionism) in favour of synchronic sociology. I argue in the next chapter that in Radcliffe-Brown's work it is especially clear that questions arising from the former perspective had to be ruled out or set aside if fruitful work along roughly Durkheimian lines was to proceed. Anthropology has come a long way since Radcliffe-Brown, but continues (in both Britain and the United States) to be constituted by the same kinds of exclusions. The dichotomy also emerged and persisted in the divergence of studies of 'acculturation' or 'social change' from functional or structural analyses of systems. The inability of a variety of traditional paradigms to integrate history with anthropology's central concerns is reflected in the fact that studies of the 'social change' genre always associate change with European contacts or some colonial presence: a definite opposition is sustained between an authentic and more or less unitary traditional entity, of great richness and cultural complexity, and on the other hand a heterogenous, relatively uninteresting and unproblematic intrusion of persons such as missionaries and settlers, and innovations such as cash crops and items of European technology. This penetration has consequences which can be examined, but these are subsequent to the culture as a primary thing which can be understood, initially, without reference to intrusions. This is what Cohn has aptly dubbed 'the missionary in the row boat' theory of change (1980: 199).

The logic of small-scale, 'tribal' or peripheral societies might alternatively be seen to be interpenetrated with this sort of colonial history in two ways: first, assuming that the ethnographer is not the first European on the scene, there are prior ways in which external change has had internal ramifications. Secondly, the structural properties of a local indigenous system can be seen to emerge in the nature of interaction with colonial forces and in particular developments. Different case histories in different areas are not just variations upon the extension of colonial influence, but are also outcomes of the differences between the social systems which are colonized.

But in most accounts there can be no continuity between the apparently messy and haphazard events of colonial history and earlier processes of 'endogenous' change, which tend not to be recognized. Although no anthropologist would now claim that a traditional society was formerly static, such a view in fact remains a premise in much anthropological writing, and particularly that concerned with hunter-gatherer societies which are frequently thought in some sense to reflect continuities from palaeolithic and neolithic epochs.[3]

The persistence of discredited ideas

These general arguments are developed in more detail in relation to particular studies. It may be thought that much of what has been said applies largely to 'out of date' perspectives in social anthropology such as functionalism, which is now notorious for its exclusion of history. We all already know that this was a flaw, so why bother discussing the problem at length? I even discuss and criticize extensively an earlier, pre-functional form of anthropology, a discourse of culture-traits or 'shreds and patches', which emerged from museums early this century – and this must seem even more distant from contemporary anthropological orientations. But in these dated visions curious ways of seeing can be detected; just as the formal element of representation is more striking in foxed nineteenth-century photographs than in yesterday's glossy snapshots. We can recognize, moreover, the continuities which our modernity seeks to write off. Part of my argument in later sections of this book is thus that recent apparently sophisticated theories – even including those attempting to capture history – have failed to shrug off in practice ideas which are discredited in so far as they are expressed. We may mention a historical context, but does that necessarily mean that it in any way animates the analysis? The argument for the exclusion of an eventful process, which was established by Radcliffe-Brown (among other functionalist writers) is no longer stated explicitly or vehemently, but since the concept of an unhistorical analysis has been developed in the practice of the discipline, perhaps such restatement has simply been unnecessary. Intellectual critique must, of course, attend to the unsaid as well as the said.

My point about anthropological discourse is thus partly that stated premises or explicit theory do not have the status which texts or scientific procedures might wish to ascribe to them; writing is like politics in the sense that unstated rationales, hidden agendas, covert classifications, and simple muddles are more important than what either the prime minister or an anthropological writer claim to be doing. Arguments come to their conclusions in disguise as often as books fail to correspond to what their authors say they are. Thus metaphors derived from contemporary political scandals are thus more useful in this epistemology than what, for example, Karl Popper has written. In particular, I stress that the absence of 'evolution' as an explicit organizing conceptual principle in much anthropology is quite misleading. The fact that most modern approaches have either actively repudiated or passively ignored or marginalized history and longer-term frameworks (of an evolutionary or diffusionist kind) strongly suggests that some sort of evolutionary scheme persists in a covert way: there are, after all, strong pressures to link particular events and cases into an overarching chronology. The problem of history is thus linked to that of evolution, and to the more general features of anthropological discourse.

The continuities between such modern perspectives as neo-Marxist regional systems theory and ways of seeing which have been long left behind, such as the dry and stilted recitation of ethnographic attributes in museum anthropology, may be unexpected and demand explanation. Here, questions of the nature of anthropological evidence are crucial. The commonsense empiricist notion is that facts have nothing to do with theory and certainly do not depend on it. This view persists in ordinary understanding and is of great consequence in some contexts such as journalism, where the motivated character of various descriptive forms is unacknowledged. However, even within the orthodox philosophy of science, this view has been extensively modified (e.g. Lakatos and Musgrave 1970). My interest is less in general propositions about such issues as the extent to which scientific observation may depend on theory, but relates rather to the particular forms which evidence may take in anthropology, and the implications of the fact that a certain sort of thing counts as 'data' to the exclusion of other things. I emphasize a much greater presence of implicit 'theory' in evidence than commonsense notions of data allow for. This point can be illustrated briefly through reference to John Beattie's work on the African kingdom of Bunyoro. One of Beattie's field methods involved organizing essay competitions for literate Nyoro on ethnographic topics such as the following:

4. '*In-law-ship*' (obuko) *and the mother's brother–sister's son relationship* (obwihwa). Explain the meanings of theses terms. Particularly, does a father-in-law respect his son-in-law ... explain how a person's mother's brothers regard and treat him. Are they allowed to be angry with him?
...
7. *Sorcery.* Say all you know about sorcery ... Discuss ... a particular case ... were the sorcerer and his victim kin, and if so what was their relationship? ...   (1965: 33)

The resulting material is not merely biased because the population must have been unevenly represented among the competitors, but, much more significantly, is moulded by the specific concerns of one phase of African structural-functionalist anthropology, and to some extent takes on the inductive, generalized form of the paradigm's anthropological description. Yet Beattie seems to have regarded these essays as a sort of raw data, and even makes the astonishing claim that such texts allowed 'the culture ... to speak for itself' (1965: 30). This is an extreme case, but comparable connections almost always exist in a more subtle form. Many recent and sophisticated ethnographies continue to privilege the words or texts of a privileged few, or even of an individual master who is charged with the enunciation of his culture (e.g. Parmentier 1987). Such expositions do not necessarily play only upon elite meanings, but the continuities between the experienced meanings of everybody's culture and the nuances of intellectual elaboration all too frequently remain hypothetical (cf. Keesing 1987). Statements of a very singular kind are thus still taken to express the properties of much more general entities. The methods of cultural anthropology therefore appear, at a general level, to be problematic; the basis for belief in particular descriptions is evidently a sort of generalized faith in the procedure of deriving insight from fieldwork, rather than any assessment of the development of particular interpretations.

Social scientists may now recognize in the context of epistemological

13

discussion that the commonsense models of data and scientific procedures are inadequate, but examination of their practice generally reveals that facts and hypotheses are developed in a way which fails to reflect an epistemology distinguishable from scientistic common nonsense. Specific 'biases', which are taken to distort the ethnography, are frequently a focal point for criticism and reinterpretation, but the overall separation between the larger corpus of evidence, and various arrays of methods and research practices, is sustained.

The significance of this for shifts and continuities in anthropological thought is that the interpretative content of past bodies of evidence is ignored or appreciated to a very limited extent. Because facts in particular genres such as museum-generated ethnography were animated by a distinct intellectual practice, the use of evidence derived from such studies in recent anthropological accounts is likely to unwittingly incorporate certain notions associated with the world view of museum anthropology. Something like this idea was, however, behind anthropologists' refusals to draw on missionary sources, which have provided the paradigm of 'biased' unprofessional description. In some diffuse and unspecified way, imputed ideas are supposed to have contaminated observation.

Writing off such sources is equivalent to refusing to read newspapers because one knows that their corporate owners have a particular view of the world which is manifest in reportage and misreportage. Of course newspapers are read by many people who at least think that they bear publishers' world views in mind, and who therefore assess the way things are put and perhaps rework them. Neither museum literature nor missionary ethnography can be dismissed *en bloc* – the genres, like journalism, may provide the only accounts available, and presumably flawed information is better than no information. Rather, 'professional' ethnographic accounts should be understood to be problematic, and something other than straightforward descriptions, to be questioned just like non-anthropological ethnography, such as is found in diverse letters home, explorers' and missionaries' narratives, and even in the motivated reports emerging from colonial administrations. In the past, the former category has enjoyed an undiscussed status, while the latter has been derided and rejected. Both need to be subjected to scrutiny and used, not simply as sources for 'ethnographic' information in the stricter sense of descriptions of customs and behaviour, but also as means to understanding the metropolitan intrusions which make observation and description possible.

The absurdity of suppressing the continuity between anthropological description and the works of such as missionaries becomes transparent if it is recalled that the transition was reflected in individual lives as much as in larger associations between discourses. Missionaries such as Maurice Leenhardt and Carl Strehlow produced celebrated examples of cultural ethnography, which have never had a secondary or merely semi-professional

14

status. Yet precisely the persistence of such an implausible boundary testifies to its significance in the scheme of anthropological meaning.

I do not develop criticisms of museum anthropology and functionalism simply because their writings reveal the mystifications and the burden of the past in contemporary anthropology. It is also important to think over and judge those earlier genres because they will continue to be deployed, not only as cases and sources within the academic discipline, but also in various ways without. Early museum ethnographies, as well as such works as Leenhardt's books on Melanesian culture in New Caledonia, are drawn into the self-representations of people with political claims and objectives.[4] If at one stage the knowledge of native cultures consciously or unconsciously served the effort toward colonial control, we now see something like the same knowledge turned toward anti-colonial or autonomist struggle. It is not the business of anthropologists to instruct the leaders of such movements, but it may be that revelations about the writing of early descriptions, and new judgements about the relationships of context and text, reflect on present political meanings. In very different circumstances, Margaret Mead's Samoan studies had implications for sex education and child-rearing in the United States; the potential ramifications in those areas of Derek Freeman's so-called refutation of her work (Freeman 1982) have not been overlooked by such bodies as the Moral Majority.

Organization of this book

In the next chapter I discuss some of the work of two major, but very different, anthropological figures in order to establish that, despite anthropology's diversity, the subject as a totality can be seen to rest upon two crucial exclusions: of history, and of the work of those lacking professional ethnographic credentials. Clearly, a discussion of two writers cannot prove this point in any technical sense, but the theorists I have chosen are representative of much wider bodies of work.

The point would be of little interest unless it could be demonstrated that the consequences of these exclusions have been detrimental. I therefore move into a more extended analysis of work on Polynesian societies, and specifically into a critique of an influential synthesis, Irving Goldman's *Ancient Polynesian society* (1970). In order to establish that an ahistorical use of ahistorical sources produces specific misinterpretations, I must go into the evidence, and sketch out reinterpretations. What I elaborate here aims only to be illustrative, as is appropriate in a work directed at anthropologists in general rather than regional specialists, but a different perspective would not be valuable unless it could deliver something different and better in the form of specific understandings.

Both my critique and reinterpretation depend largely on sources which do not belong to modern anthropology, but stem rather from the ventures and incursions of missionaries, explorers and others. The status of such accounts is of fundamental importance to historical anthropology: the orientation of the whole exercise depends on judgements about their value, about the issues that they bear upon. I therefore review some of the writings: the point is not so much that anthropology has generally failed to acknowledge that these early accounts sometimes contain reasonable synchronic ethnographic descriptions, but rather that they refer to events which have often had a crucial impact on culture. It is segregation of a systemic entity, 'culture' or 'society', from the sorts of events studied by historians, which I argue cannot be sustained.

This evaluation leads into discussion of another kind of evolutionary theory, to an approach which refuses to acknowledge the initial opposition of structure and time. This is the form of neo-Marxist regional systems theory developed in the work of Ekholm and Friedman. The theory is found to be more satisfactory in its premises than its application to the Pacific, but suggestions about the links between longer-term processes in local social evolution and changes consequent upon European contact point to a crucial shift towards the integration of the central systemic concerns of anthropology and apparently contingent histories – the sort of integration which the fundamental society–event opposition has generally precluded. But these attempts are by no means unproblematic, as discussion of their implications for Polynesia reveals. It may surprise some readers that I pay so much attention to what perhaps seems merely one of a number of attempts to refine or expand the disintegrated paradigm of neo-Marxist anthropology. But although Ekholm's work has not been widely appraised, I argue that it has substantial implications for the wider anthropological endeavour because it actively displaces classical evolution with another longer time-frame – a systemic history which can integrate structural transformations and events. The importance of this step derives from the fact that evolutionary types and conceptions often persist under the surface in anthropological theories which do not appear to be evolutionary in orientation. In order to definitively and effectively break from what (almost) everybody regards as discredited, we must make this kind of explicit theoretical shift.

In producing more historical analyses, we do not want, however, to abandon the insights generated by former anthropological paradigms, and particularly those produced by symbolic analyses. Is it possible to reconstruct such perspectives in a more historical mode? In a reading of some recent studies by Marshall Sahlins, I discuss another attempt to integrate structure and history – parallel to that of Ekholm, except that in these cases the structures are of a structuralist kind, and history turns out to retain a more contingent character. I attempt to demonstrate the proposition stated above, that these sophisticated and novel theories carry a burden of undisclosed

16

theory which is neither sophisticated nor novel; particularly, they embody various notions of an evolutionary kind which no-one would want to sustain. The dependence on ideas of evolutionary change which are not merely unspecified but are actually analytically submerged suggests that it is in fact necessary to rework an explicit theory of history or evolution; however, the models of change offered by Sahlins do not make longer-term structural transformation possible. Together with the fact that his arguments are far more applicable to early contact history than to later stages of colonial confrontation, this indicates the need for different models for different historical time-scales. Sahlins does make some crucial gains, especially in the structural analysis of temporal processes, but does leave the interconnections of meaningful orders and colonial histories unexplored. A perspective integrating these different historic time-scales – which perhaps would also speak more directly to contemporary problems in colonial and post-colonial societies – cannot be arrived at without revision of anthropological method, both at the levels of analytic procedure through contextualization, and in the practices of gathering evidence. One of the crucial steps would be the decentring of ethnographic fieldwork as the source of anthropological knowledge.

I thus begin by working out some 'epistemological' points in the context of evolutionary argument, and proceed to developments of evolutionary and historical analysis which demand reconstruction at an epistemological level. Half the point of this tangle is an insistence on the indissociable relation of these different aspects of knowledge – which are certainly not connected in the neat hierarchy envisaged in empiricist commonsense.

2

Radcliffe-Brown, Geertz and the foundations of modern anthropology

... he eschewed guesswork history (one must add, all history).
Evans-Pritchard (1981)

The question must arise of how writing about others, about society and culture, became ahistorical in the first place. The histories of British and American anthropology – to which I have felt obliged to confine myself – are separate, and a full exploration of the issue would require a much longer work. In the United States, the Boasian school insisted, in opposition to evolutionism, upon the plurality of cultures and the complexity of specific historical and geographic influences upon their development. 'History' was thus not excluded, but was definitely understood in diffusionist terms: the suggestion that an institution, or some feature of social organization, had come from elsewhere was a form of explanation. However, the trend in the work of Lowie, Mead, Radin and Benedict, as well as in others who were not students of Boas, such as Murdock, was for analysis to revolve around a mixture of comparative, psychological and functional concerns. 'History', in diffusionist terms, played a part, but gradually became less and less significant, so that although recent American anthropology is inflected – in the context of many other influences – by a Boasian background, general features, such as the overall orientation toward relativism, are far more significant than any residual interest in diffusionism (for much more extensive discussion, see e.g. Stocking 1968).

I argue later, in relation to the Bishop Museum's variant of American anthropology, that this Boasian approach in fact tended to actively obscure history, but here I simply point out that the insistence upon the 'historical' singularity of each group did not necessarily entail any interest in recent history, or in the current circumstances of the people who were the subject of ethnological investigation. But since even this unhistorical 'history' tended to go out of fashion, in its later development American cultural anthropology did not differ substantially in this respect from its transatlantic counterpart. So, in the second part of this chapter, I argue that what one of the founders of the British school was so assertive about, is implicit in the analysis of a very different writer. The point here is not to argue that Geertz and Radcliffe-Brown are more similar in their theoretical views than has been previously recognized, but that some features of anthropological discourse

18

are so fundamental that they are manifested in writings which are otherwise utterly different. Particularly, elements of early work, which are heavily criticized and widely rejected, persist in contemporary writing which continues to be highly influential. It would not be worth discussing Radcliffe-Brown at length, if he had not expressed overtly what continues to be sustained between the lines.

A. R. Radcliffe-Brown was the dominant theorist of the British structural-functional school and, as such, was one of the most influential anthropologists of this century.[1] Unlike the other founder figure, Malinowski, his ethnographic contributions were far less significant than a series of pithy essays which expounded a positivistic sociology of functional regularities, especially in the domain of 'social organization' or kinship structure. The breaking up of the structural-functional perspective in the 1960s naturally saw his stature diminish, and some more recent judgements of his contribution have been harsh.[2]

His work was nevertheless crucial because, along with Malinowski's, it stands as one of the foundations of what is understood as modern anthropology. While histories of the subject discuss many earlier writers, such as Lafitau, Montesquieu, Morgan, Tylor, Frazer and others, these men are usually regarded by contemporary anthropologists (when they are regarded at all) as precursors. Although some developed ideas which may still be interesting, the essential feature of the modern profession has always been seen as the elaboration of theory or interpretation on the basis of extended empirical research. This conjunction was not found in writers before Malinowski and Radcliffe-Brown.[3] The shift in method towards fieldwork paralleled a break from evolutionary and diffusionist speculation in favour of a scientific, law-seeking functionalism – or such was the received picture.

It has been argued that Radcliffe-Brown was the first 'real professional' in British social anthropology, because he was professionally trained, paid to be an anthropologist, taught and trained others, conducted his activities within institutional frameworks, and wrote for an audience of professional colleagues rather than the lay public.[4] Different criteria could, of course, be used to identify earlier professional ethnologists, and the definitional issue is not really important in itself. What is significant, however, is that Radcliffe-Brown's effort to establish a 'natural science of society' was effected through a series of exclusions which have had far-reaching consequences in the discipline. These were, essentially, the rejection of any kind of historical causality, and the rejection of pre-professional ethnographic research.

A science must have a tightly defined object of study. If it is to appear rigorous and effective, it must also be able to generate explanations within its domain. From a positivistic perspective which seeks to generalize about primitive societies or society as such, a loose view of causality which acknowledges the importance of particular circumstances and myriad anterior causes is anathema: such a lack of boundedness and fixity must completely undermine the effort to specify tight relationships and laws. Radcliffe-Brown's mature approach was accurately summarised by Eggan: 'a limited number of structural principles [are] isolated by comparative study of diverse systems and shown to underly a variety of social and cultural phenomena' (1949: 121). At least in theory, the method thus has no need to appeal to phenomena or causes beyond the clear boundaries of its own field of vision: society. There is no dependence on any other science such as biology or geography for essential elements of an understanding, and the discourse appears to be autonomous and rigorous. The ramifications of these issues are, of course, not simply intellectual, as research funding and institutional status have always been affected by the self-presentations of various competing subjects, the bias usually being towards those which appear 'harder' and more like the natural sciences.

Professional foundations: the exclusion of happenings

The first work of Radcliffe-Brown's in which his perspective was presented was *The Andaman Islanders*, written before the first world war but not published until 1922. In some ways it was a transitional work, since the apprentice research upon which it was based was directed as much at an old-fashioned description of culture traits, technology and physical anthropology as the study of social organization. The state of ideas at the time of the fieldwork (1905–6) was reflected in an appendix on 'The technical culture of the Andaman Islanders' (1922: 407–94), but two substantial chapters were dedicated to the elaboration of what the author saw as 'a new method in the interpretation of the institutions of a primitive people' (1922: ix). These begin with a dismissal of the diffusionists who saw themselves as explaining institutions in one place on the basis of links with other populations or migrations; this kind of 'hypothetical reconstruction of the past [was] of very doubtful utility' (1922: 229). Moreover, events in the past which could not be known with certainty did not 'provide suitable material from which to draw generalizations' (1922: 229 n1). The appropriate problems were thus 'not historical but psychological or sociological'; the project was not conjectural history but the 'social physiology' of a 'general system of ideas and sentiments' or 'customs' (1922: 230).

The sort of 'historical' writing which Radcliffe-Brown had in mind was often interested in establishing entirely contrived connections between one group and some civilized centre such as Egypt or India on the basis of similarities which were both arbitrarily selected and often only superficial. The attack upon these implausible and peculiarly motivated efforts still seems justified, but it must be noted that their inadequacy does not in itself establish the irrelevance of past events to the functioning of a social system – no more than the fact that some evidence bearing upon a crime has been misrepresented or irretrievably lost somehow makes that category of evidence subsequently worthless.[5]

As Evans-Pritchard succinctly noted, Radcliffe-Brown effectively assimilated all history to that which could only be imperfectly known and excluded it from the field of analysis. This was a critical step for social anthropology, because it sealed off the domain of social organization or culture from that of recent historical change, which permitted the development of apparently coherent explanation within the former domain. The persisting salience of this move is evident from the fact that more recent writers continue to contrapose modern, soundly-based studies to evolutionist or diffusionist speculation (e.g. La Fontaine 1985: 20–2). However, the analyses which stemmed from this departure were arguably flawed precisely because history was ignored.

Radcliffe-Brown did not pretend that European contact had had no influence on the Andamanese: in the introduction he described the impact of a penal settlement at Port Blair upon the indigenous population, noting changes in residence patterns, mobility and depopulation (1922: 10–18). However, in the subsequent chapter he proceeded to stress that 'what is really of interest to the ethnologist is the social organisation of these tribes as it existed before the European occupation of the islands'. Despite 'extensive' changes, it was 'fairly easy...to discover from the natives themselves what was the constitution of their society in former times' (1922: 22). This claim may be questioned. The penal settlement was established in 1858; from the indigenous point of view this seems to have been a critical if not catastrophic moment qualitatively different from any earlier foreign intrusion. There was great hostility at first, and it might therefore be supposed that Radcliffe-Brown's informants would have had a clear sense of this dividing line and have understood that he wanted information about their undisturbed, pre-Port Blair existence. It is difficult to know, however, the extent to which the informants would have been able to provide accurate information about the situation fifty years earlier. There was in any case a distillation of memory and observation, so that it is no longer clear what information might relate to 1858 and what might be more a part of an ethnography of a later, colonized society.[6] Although Radcliffe-Brown's Durkheimian analysis depended precisely upon the exclusion of the contingent happenings of colonial history, a cursory examination tends to reveal the Andamanese situation partly as a product of forces beyond the neat domain of 'social organization'. For example, the indigenous ethnic distinctions are mostly spoken of as though they had deep roots in ancient linguistic and cultural differentiation, but the separateness of the Jarawa of south Andaman appears to have been magnified if not created through contrasting patterns of indigenous resistance. They seem to have been different principally because they were more hostile, but this state was represented by several writers as an attribute of their more savage nature, although one British administrator observed that they 'seem to be very much what we have made them' (Portman 1899, II: 711). 'Jarawa' in fact appears not to be a tribal name, but was probably a term meaning enemies or strangers used by the groups which the British had initial contact with, and was applied to certain other groups apart from those subsequently categorized as 'Jarawa' (cf. Portman 1899, I: 76). Radcliffe-Brown in fact acknowledges this in passing (1922: 10), but proceeds to treat the distinction as though it had as much historical depth as that between French and English.

Further issues arise if involvement with foreigners before 1858 is taken into account. There were many centuries of sporadic contact, which were probably of limited significance, but ships' visits and shipwrecks became more frequent in the first half of the nineteenth century. By 1771 the Andamanese were 'aware of the value of iron' and between 1789 and 1796 there was an unsuccessful attempt to establish a colony (*ibid*: 9–10). Portman (1899) mentions other more or less violent incidents of early contact, too numerous to be reviewed here. The histories of other places would suggest that such events as these had social and cultural ramifications, but for Radcliffe-Brown there was no link between the summary history of his introduction and the real subject-matter of ethnology.

Professional foundations: the monopoly over competence

The second exclusion which was crucial to the establishment of professional anthropology was that of amateur observers. The need for this was obvious, since funding for training professional observers could hardly be justified if one acknowledged that others could do or had done the job of ethnographic description just as well. There was also a sense that writing about a place was usually of little value unless it was directly concerned with ethnographic subjects: the vital data did not emerge in a marginal way from other descriptive materials.

Because Radcliffe-Brown experienced various difficulties in his fieldwork in the Andamans (Langham 1981: 247f.), he was obliged to draw on some articles by the administrator E. H. Man, which had been published in the *Journal of the Anthropological Institute* in the 1880s, although at several points he insinuated that Man's observations or interpretations were less than convincing (e.g. 1922: 266, 370 n1). Other works, however, are swept aside: it is noted that M. V. Portman wrote a book called *A history of our relations with the Andamanese*; this 'contains a mass of information on the subject with which it deals, but does not add very much to our knowledge of the Andamanese themselves' (*ibid*: 21). Anyone who cares to consult this book, which Radcliffe-Brown scarcely cites subsequently, will discover that this statement is a gross misrepresentation. The work in fact contains a great deal of information on tribal divisions, initiation, marriage, greeting customs, and many other 'ethnological' matters; some of this information is in a discursive form, but there is much else scattered through accounts of many particular events. Another book, F. J. Mouat's *Adventures and researches among the Andaman Islanders* (1863), also contains much detail but is only referred to once (1922: 27).

In these cases earlier writers are mostly denigrated through being ignored, but in his later work on Australian Aboriginal social organisation, Radcliffe-Brown felt confident enough to take a more aggressive tone toward those whom he apparently saw as pre-scientific amateurs. He found most earlier accounts 'inaccurate', 'misleading' and 'so lacking in precision as to be almost useless' (1931: 33–4), and proceeded to note that Howitt's and R. H. Mathews' work, being derived from 'decidedly unreliable' informants, could not 'be accepted without careful criticism'; Howitt was 'often responsible for much confusion' (*ibid*: 33, cf. 52, 55, 56, 66); an account of Spencer and Gillen's was 'probably inaccurate' (*ibid*: 49); another passage of their writing was 'not as precise as might be desired' (*ibid*: 76, 78); Roth's lists of kinship terms were 'not very satisfactory' (*ibid*: 70); his description of another area 'incomplete and confused' (*ibid*: 69, cf. 71–2). I am prepared to believe that many of these texts are in fact more or less seriously flawed, but what is notable about Radcliffe-Brown's style is the absence of justification for these aspersions. Despite the fact that *The social organization of Australian tribes* is a highly technical monograph which goes into considerable detail about names and classifications, these condemnations of other people's evidence are pronounced constantly but not supported in detail: the suggestion that Howitt's and Mathews' informants were unreliable is one of the most specific claims, but it is not revealed to the reader why these informants were less reliable than any others. The charges are quite unsubstantiated.[7]

What the criticisms ignore is the fact that any description prepared with one set of questions in mind will necessarily be at least slightly inadequate to the purposes of another set of interests. A highly sophisticated 1980s ethnography of cultural categories might be based on the most searching fieldwork, yet be 'so lacking in precision as to be almost useless' in resolving questions about a distinct topic such as agricultural production. A dedicated and sympathetic exercise in interpretation, which took the premises of refractory texts into account, might in fact turn their observations toward other purposes, but it would be unfair to expect Radcliffe-Brown's scientism to countenance or even think of such a hermeneutic exercise: description was simply either good or bad; there was clarity or confusion.

The tone of what may as well be called smears might lead one to make

23

assumptions about Radcliffe-Brown's personal style or arrogance (e.g. Langham 1981: 250–3, 290–1), but, apart from leading one into matters of limited significance for anthropological theory, this would ignore the systematic, discursive effect of such persistently disparaging comments and allusions. The repetitive and generalized character of the criticisms suggests that there was another implicit project beyond the clarification of Aboriginal social groupings in Radcliffe-Brown's book.[8] This sense is reinforced by the work's final paragraph:

> My chief purpose has been to remove certain misconceptions about the Australian social organization that are current in anthropological literature and thus to clear the way forward for a sociological study of the Australian culture. As a result of the researches carried out during the last four years by Lloyd Warner, Elkin, Miss McConnel, Hart, Thomson and Piddington, researches which it is hoped will be continued, it is now possible to undertake that study with some hope of reaching valid and important conclusions. (1931: 124)

The value of clearing the ground may be self-evident, but it is unfortunate that this agricultural or colonizing metaphor is reminiscent of the activities of the white settlers who displaced Aboriginal landowners and created a vacant space for their own projects and achievements. The cumulative effect of Radcliffe-Brown's allegations is to discredit a whole generation of writers, to suggest that disentangling their usage is an unprofitable exercise, that their works are better set aside, and attention focussed on the proper research which was only just beginning. A discursive space was indeed being colonized.

This is not to say that the work of Radcliffe-Brown embodies the origin or sole origin of the conditions of professional talk, since such moves were made by many other anthropologists, both minor and influential, whose work straddled the interface between the supposedly pre-scientific and professional phases of the discipline. These exclusions, moreover, are not simply steps which were taken in the formation of structural-functional anthropology, but persist, mostly implicitly, as premises in both cultural and social anthropology in general. In Radcliffe-Brown's discourse the exclusions which create the anthropological space are pronounced loudly. In later writers, they are usually not, because that space was already securely constituted.

Cultural anthropology: implicit exclusions

Who could be more distant from Radcliffe-Brown than humanist, culturalist and relativist Clifford Geertz, who has envisaged and promoted 'not an experimental science in search of law but an interpretive one in search of meaning' (1973: 5)? So far as interests and style are concerned, everything differs, but in certain crucial respects there is a common frame of discourse.

24

Geertz's anthropology is characterized by a method of elucidation, rather than theory. The general propositions and terms are thus very vague; culture is a text (but how is a text conceived?); religion is a system of symbols (but then, everything is symbolic).[9] The strength of the analysis is not, however, intended to arise from the elaboration of abstractions, but from an interpretive working-out of the flow of social discourse in particular contexts – and, of course, it is in such grounded essays as 'Deep play' on Balinese cockfights that Geertz's talents are expressed.

An important feature of the perspective is a very close identification between the elaboration of anthropological understanding and the practice of ethnography. Thick, culturally rich, contextualized description is arrived at through fieldwork.[10] What is crucial is the 'kind of intellectual effort' this is: 'sorting out the structures of significance... and determining their social ground and import' (1973: 9). This process of analysis is directly identified with the (partial) establishment of social and cultural competence in the foreign[11] situation.

Finding our feet, an unnerving business which never more than distantly succeeds, is what ethnographic research consists of as a personal experience; trying to formulate the basis on which one imagines, always excessively, one has found them is what anthropological writing consists of as scientific endeavour. (1973: 13)

The effect of these propositions is a monopolization of the field of thick description or cultural interpretation – set up as the proper terrain of anthropology – by professional ethnographers: only they undergo the appropriate experience, make the distinctive 'intellectual effort', which provides the basis for this interpretive quest. Apparently those whose feet have always been on the ground are not equipped to articulate the sentences of their 'public document' and it seems obvious that historians, geographers and others concerned in one way or another with social and cultural analysis have no part either in this grand endeavour toward 'the enlargement of the universe of human discourse' (1973: 14) – or if they contribute, it is not on the basis of the ground we anthropologists have marked out. This approach to the subject thus excludes both those who analyse or theorize without ethnographic experience and those who experience without ethnographic credentials. The exclusion is less prominent in Geertz's discourse than the insults are in Radcliffe-Brown, because Geertz inhabits an anthropological world which is already professionalized, from which amateurs are already excluded. The boundary can thus be implicitly reproduced, and does not need to be actively created by displacing predecessors and denigrating their work.

Geertz's analysis operates essentially by identifying vital symbols, important oppositions, themes, or concerns in the culture studied and relating an array of acts or other features to whatever has been initially

25

singled out. The identification between Balinese men and their cocks is the basis for an explication of why the literal and figurative stakes in cockfighting can be high, how personal antagonisms make them higher, why cocks from allied groups rather than the same group face each other, and so on (1973: 437f.). Similarly, 'certain central ideas' which reduce to contrasts between inside/outside and refined/vulgar define 'the Javanese sense of what a person is' (1983: 60). The approach is problematic because the arguments usually *start with* a claim that something is a key symbol or 'central idea'. Such assertions presumably have a basis in what is inferred from speech or about thought, but this is not explained. However, such issues are of less concern than the formal sense in which this analysis is virtually the same as Radcliffe-Brown's: to modify Eggan's characterization a limited number of cultural principles are isolated somehow and shown to underly a variety of social and cultural phenomena. The analysis thus operates by selecting certain features within a social or cultural domain and demonstrating their consistency or coherence with others. In a sociological functionalism, this entails establishing that an institution plays a part such as providing an outlet for social tensions; in 'interpretive anthropology' it involves showing that some meanings are versions of others, that an act can be understood to express a meaning, and so on. While *concepts* of time may interest both perspectives, historical time has no place in either.

However, Geertz's exclusion of history is somewhat more complicated than Radcliffe-Brown's, even though its conceptual absence might be presumed from its absence in his general discussions of the nature of anthropology. The difference arises partly from the difference between the Indonesian and north African societies studied by Geertz and the Andaman Islanders, who in fact correspond to the stereotype of tribal ethnography: the people were encountered for the first time by Europeans a couple of centuries or even just a few decades ago; prior to that, everything is obscure; in effect, there is no history. This is in any case convenient, because anthropologists want to treat their customs and beliefs as elements of a unitary, timeless system, and the idea is most convincing if one thinks of the system as having operated in an autonomous, undisturbed way for a long time. Of course, so much is known (in general if not specifically) about population movements, the spread of world religions, the extensive dynamics of ancient trading systems, and long histories of interaction with European powers, that such notions could not be entertained with respect to such places as Morocco, Java and Bali. (And this is true of most of Asia, the Middle East, north Africa, Mesoamerica, and of course Europe.) However, the dynamics are acknowledged without being linked to the category of 'culture'. The multiplicity of influences is seen as a backdrop which injects richness and complexity into the present situation (e.g. Geertz 1968: 42–8; Tambiah 1970: 25).

In his famous essay on a Javanese ritual and social change, Geertz raised the question of the difficulties posed for functionalism by social change and history. He proposed, however, that these problems can be dealt with if society and culture are clearly distinguished and seen as 'independently variable yet mutually interdependent' (1973: 144): neither side of experience should be reduced or subordinated to the other. Briefly, the article describes how factors such as the differences between a partly secularized political party and Islam generated a crisis at a boy's funeral. Rites which were meaningful were spoilt because they had also come to be signifiers in a larger ideological struggle. The explanation turns on the discrepancy between cultural and social circumstances: the people were partly integrated into urban society, with its patterns of work, stratification, and political life, but culturally they essentially inhabited the world of rural villagers:

The patterns of belief, expression and value to which the kampong man is committed – his world view, ethos, ethic, or whatever – differ only slightly from those followed by the villager. Amid a radically more complex social environment, he clings noticeably to the symbols which guided him or his parents through life in rural society. And it is this fact which gave rise to the psychological and social tension surrounding Paidjan's funeral. (1973: 165)

The analysis in fact says nothing about history or time but rather uses change as a mechanism to isolate the incompleteness of systems. Clearly, if functional theory was entirely adequate, social occasions such as the funeral would never go horribly wrong as this one did. If meanings were all effectively shared, confusions and mistakes of this kind should not happen. The problems created for an analysis which sees people acting out culture as though it were a coherent public document can be constrained if a specific source of incoherence is situated in the gap between the social and cultural aspects of life. The coherence of both domains is potentially preserved; both can be analysed as systems without reference to time. History simply sometimes provides the source of discrepancy between the two; there is certainly no interest in historicizing culture itself.

The apparent openness to history of Geertz's anthropology is thus entirely illusory. Although very different to British structural analysis, and obviously an advance upon it, so far as matters of culture and meaning are concerned, certain underlying features of the discourse are the same. The discipline may thus have put a crude positivism and much else in Radcliffe-Brown behind it, but it has not effectively shrugged off the crucial exclusions which interpretive anthropology, and a variety of other recent schools, continue to presuppose. What is required now is a fuller demonstration of the ways in which these exclusions are actually damaging.

3

The background to Polynesian anthropology

Criticism of the ahistorical character of anthropological accounts would be relatively uninteresting if it simply revealed that this blindness gave rise to sporadic errors. Strictly theoretical criticism would be equally unimportant if it failed to establish that an approach free of the alleged fault would generate novel understandings of particular cases. I thus attempt to establish that various particular mistakes have systematic features which can only be explained through a more general critique, and moreover that this critique makes more powerful reinterpretation possible. This – together with my argument that the distance between theories and evidence is illusory – requires that the argument moves constantly between apparently theoretical and apparently substantive issues, between general subterfuges and particular explanations.

I have chosen one body of anthropological writing for discussion in detail. This is the literature concerned with Polynesia, and particularly with social evolution and transformation in that region. This material is especially relevant to more general issues of the status of history and anthropological epistemology, because discussion has been dominated by the interpretation of traditional variation within the 'culture area' in transformational terms of one kind or another. The debates have demanded or presumed a knowledge of traditional systems, but in all cases the societies changed dramatically between the period of early contact with explorers and the time of professional observation. The question of quite what is being compared is thus problematic. One sort of historical time tends therefore to be excluded from (evolutionist) models which are ostensibly about temporal, diachronic processes. The peculiar formulations of unashamedly evolutionist arguments – which are somewhat discredited in contemporary anthropological culture – are found to permeate quite different, non-evolutionist, paradigms. A cluster of contradictions associated with the preoccupation with the traditional despite history thus emerges very clearly in the Polynesian case (but is hardly specific to it). The existence of a substantial corpus of early twentieth-century ethnography, as well as substantial and diverse bodies of earlier documentation, permits me to pursue the issue, alluded to above, of the status of different forms of evidence in shifting theoretical perspectives. The status of history is, of course, linked in the closest possible way to notions of the worth of historical sources, and the significance of the problems such sources tend to speak to.

The unity of Polynesia

The comparative orientation of Polynesian anthropology effectively highlights questions of the nature of the anthropological entities, such as local 'cultures', which constitute the units to be compared. This orientation itself arises from the perception of Polynesia as a diverse but fundamentally unitary area. This view developed originally in the course of Captain Cook's expeditions, which visited most of the larger island groups, and initiated contact with many. The physical similarities between the 'copper-coloured' people were notable, but a great deal else could be seen to be shared: the cultivation of root crops such as yams and taro; an orientation towards the sea manifested in a variable reliance on fishing, and well-constructed canoes; items of material culture – found to some extent in common forms and designs – such as adzes, bark cloth, and wooden bowls, which were collected by early voyagers in great quantities; and elaborate deference and rank distinctions associated with 'kings' and 'royal' families. The understanding of indigenous religion was especially uneven in the late eighteenth century, but notions of 'taboo' and 'superior beings' (Cook [1967]: 179) were recognized to be pervasive.[1]

The postulation of unity facilitated internal comparison, and discussion of variants on the basis of better known cases. In the introductory matter to the account of the voyage of the *Duff* (which between 1796 and 1798 established the first evangelical missions in the Pacific) it is explained that, 'to avoid tautology' (i.e. repetition) in the brief descriptions of various islands, 'the points wherein they vary from Otaheite are principally insisted on' (Wilson 1799: vi). There is subsequently much comparative discussion: the Tongans 'had less cloth, but more matting than the Georgian Islanders' (i.e. the Tahitians); 'the power of the chiefs is more despotic at Tongataboo, although exercised with less outrage to private property' (*ibid*: xlix, liii; cf. 383–6). Johann Reinhold Forster, who accompanied Cook on his second voyage, subsequently published a discursive work (1778) which contained some four hundred pages of comparative ethnographic discussion of this kind. The pattern of divergence in unity emerged most directly from the discussion of language. It was immediately apparent that many words, such as *ariki* (chief), *mate* (sickness, death), *kai* (food), and the numbers were the same or similar across wide areas (Banks [1962] II: 35–7). It was further noted that the differences partly reflected regular consonant shifts: *tapu* became *kapu* in Hawaiian, *tangata* (Maori for person) *kanaka*, and so on. These variations were frequently illustrated in tabular form – most ex-

29

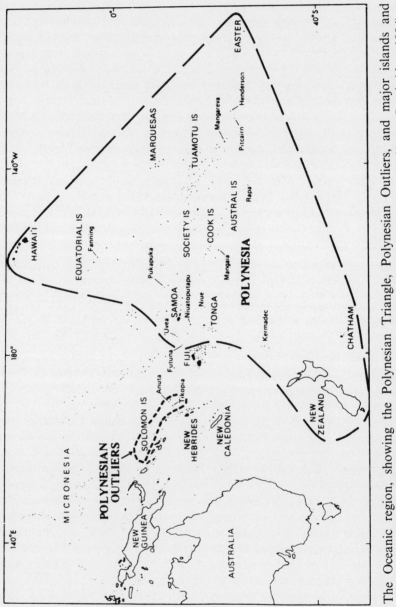

The Oceanic region, showing the Polynesian Triangle, Polynesian Outliers, and major islands and archipelagos (from Patrick Vinton Kirch, *The evolution of the Polynesian chiefdoms*, Cambridge, 1984).

tensively by Forster – and reflect the most systematic aspect of the early European understanding of Polynesia.

The idea was thus that one 'race' or 'nation' had spread itself across the Pacific, reaching 'the large country of *New Zealand*' and even having made 'a surprising stretch to the solitary spot called *Easter Island*'. These 'astonishing migrations' were thought by some to have arisen 'from designs of conquest' (Wilson 1799: lxxxv; cf. Cook [1961]: 354). All this is described in a very eighteenth-century way, but the basic insights remain far more credible than those of any other diffusionist scheme. Modern linguistic and archaeological research has strengthened and specified the notion that the inhabitants of the various Polynesian islands are descended from a group speaking an Austronesian language in eastern Melanesia which moved into Fiji and western Polynesia before 3,000 years ago – although continuity rather than 'racial' difference with Melanesia would now be stressed (Bellwood 1978; Kirch 1984; Kirch and Green 1987).

The significance of an apparently isolated region of discrete island societies which were at once closely related yet distinct in specific ways was not lost for long on speculative social theorists:

The Islands of the South Seas present a spectacle of extraordinary interest to the moral and political philosopher. While certain principles of polity are common to them all, there are striking diversities everywhere apparent. Organization existed in various degrees of completeness, and despotism in divers states of strength; and both might be taken as the index of the exact stage that a people had reached in the march towards civilization. (Campbell 1840: 474)

The darker skin, less-civilized appearance, and absence of hierarchical organization among the inhabitants of New Holland (Australia), New Guinea, New Caledonia, and so on, made them seem clearly different to the Polynesians to the east. However, the distinction between the two regions was less sharply drawn in the late eighteenth and nineteenth centuries: the whole area was usually alluded to as 'the South Seas' and Melanesian islands such as those comprising the New Hebrides (now Vanuatu) and New Caledonia were often called 'western Polynesia'. The rigidified Melanesia–Polynesia opposition, defined in its modern form by Dumont D'Urville (1832; cf. Hale 1846), became much more widely accepted around the beginning of this century: the Fijian group, which was clearly a somewhat embarrassing overlap, marked the easternmost part of Melanesia, everything beyond that being Polynesia, which of course included New Zealand. An equally spurious boundary was drawn between the Ellice Islands (now Tuvalu) and 'Micronesian' atolls to the north-west.

The notion that the Polynesian populations were racially distinct from their darker neighbours to the west prompted a great deal of diffusionist speculation about their 'origins', which were traced to various higher south-east Asian civilizations. The more extravagant varieties of this literature blossomed in the late nineteenth and early twentieth centuries (e.g. Fornander 1878–80) but the set of concerns persisted in more restrained archaeological discussion until recently.

Much nineteenth-century writing on the Pacific was more localized, drawing on personal knowledge rather than library snippets, and only indirectly reflecting larger evolutionist or diffusionist conceptions. Some books, such as the missionary George Turner's *Samoa a hundred years ago and long before* (1884), were primarily discursive accounts of beliefs and mythology; others, like William Churchward's *My consulate in Samoa* (1887), revolved more around an individual's experiences and observations (in that case, from an official's perspective).

Twentieth-century anthropological perceptions

The anthropological knowledge of Polynesia as a region is unusual in that until recently it derived less from a haphazard array of individual studies done at different times than from a systematic effort by one body – the Honolulu-based Bishop Museum, which aimed to describe all Polynesian cultures. The effort began in 1920 and carried on through the thirties. The emphasis in research and publication was manifestly on data rather than interpretation, but an underlying diffusionist framework was occasionally made more explicit (e.g. Handy 1930). This perspective was strongest amongst ethnologists such as Peter Buck and E. S. C. Handy who were permanently associated with the museum; work was also published by others such as Alfred Métraux and Margaret Mead who had different concerns but a broadly similar Boasian and particularist orientation. Raymond Firth's monumental sequence of Tikopia studies was exceptional in that it was one of very few British structural-functional contributions to Polynesian anthropology.[2] It was also unusual in that the ethnographic vision was focussed virtually exclusively on the society studied: although Firth used the ethnography to discuss general anthropological issues in many papers, references to comparative Polynesian materials and debates are few and far between.

In the 1950s anthropologists to whom scientific metaphors came naturally began to speak of Polynesia as a 'laboratory' for studies of controlled comparison (Goodenough 1957). This was, of course, a refinement of the sort of notion enunciated by John Campbell in 1840. The perception was applied in the fullest way by Marshall Sahlins in his early book *Social stratification in Polynesia* (1958) which drew on the ecological perspectives of Leslie White and Julian Steward. Sahlins argued that the Polynesian societies could be divided into two categories, 'ramage systems' and 'descent line systems', which reflected ecological adaptations to different island types. This study was very influential in American neo-evolutionary anthropology, but was widely criticized on empirical grounds. At about the same time Irving Goldman (1955) put forward an argument from a less determinist perspective, emphasizing aristocratic competition (or 'status rivalry') which was seen to produce a pattern of evolutionary changes in leadership, social organization and rank distinctions. The article was subsequently expanded into *Ancient Polynesian society* (1970), which added a mass of detail but retained a relatively simple overall thesis. In the longer run neither Sahlins' nor Goldman's core arguments have stood up, although elements of both retain currency. Sahlins' early work perhaps suffered particularly from changing theoretical fashions, since the vigorous ecological materialism the book typified only retained credibility among archaeologists, some of whom have also, more recently, adopted a more 'social' perspective, while maintaining an interest in larger processes of development and trans-formation (Kirch 1984, 1986 [ed.]).

A history of Polynesian studies – which this book is not – would have to discuss many other writers and particular tendencies. If the regional specialists' debate about Sahlins' 1958 book had not already been exhaustive, a critique of evolutionary analysis would have to pay as much attention to that as to the work of Goldman. *Ancient Polynesian society* is in some ways an intricate work, and certainly is one which reveals the ambiguities and elisions inherent in the encounter between one sort of anthropology and a problematic body of evidence. Primarily for this reason, but also because there is still no clear consensus as to how substantial a contribution Goldman's book in fact is, I discuss it, rather than *Social stratification in Polynesia*, at some length. Sahlins' book however suffered from many of the same weaknesses in the use of sources, and one line of my general argument – that ahistorical biases in evidence have ramifications for subsequent interpretation – could have been developed in relation to either work.

Goldman's main sources were the ethnographic bulletins of the Bishop Museum – which also were used by many other writers, such as those who drew the more centralized Polynesian societies into models of the development of the 'early' state (e.g. Claessen and Skalnik 1981; Service 1975; cf. Ortner 1981). I therefore go back to these and attempt to tease out some of the more general concepts behind museum anthropology, specifically the ideas relating to the constitution of the object of 'native culture' and the sorts of evidence which have a bearing on it. Some of these arguments could be extended to other bodies of museum anthropology, such as the Siberian and North American Indian work of the American Museum of Natural History (much of which was more directly controlled or influenced by Boas) – but it is not my purpose to delineate the contours of the whole genre.[3] The point is rather that there are complicit relations of theory and evidence in these texts which offer themselves as mere reports; the implicit interpreta-tions, which are not really separable from the evidence, are inherited by other writers who draw from these data quarries. This process whereby a covert analysis is transmitted into another account is examined through Goldman's use of a bulletin concerning the Marquesas Islands. The other side of this argument is a positive reinterpretation of some patterns of change in eastern Polynesia; this establishes that a different use of evidence can demand a distinct evolutionary model, and, more specifically, that the use of archaeological evidence can help bypass one of the most general problems of evolutionary anthropology – namely, that while it pretends to deal with temporal processes it in fact does little more than use temporal metaphors to make discriminations within certain kinds of comparative or classificatory social models.

4

An evolutionary argument and its sources

The societies of the Pacific Islands and especially Polynesia have often been used to illustrate arguments about social evolution and, in cases such as Hawaii, the development of 'early' states. Irving Goldman's *Ancient Polynesian society* was the most sustained study of this kind; it attempted a detailed analysis of evidence concerning eighteen Polynesian groups, and formulated evolutionary categories more founded on local variation than universal schema. Much of Goldman's massive work consisted of presentation and discussion of evidence relating to the eighteen societies he studied. Although questions were raised about sources and interpretations by specialists (Howard 1972), *Ancient Polynesian society* rapidly acquired the status of a sourcebook on Polynesia, which (as one writer expressed it) did 'much to document and clarify' the Polynesian societies (Friedman 1981: 278).[1] The perhaps unfashionable character of the argument thus does not detract from the book's continuing influence in shaping academic perceptions of the region. Some sections of the text consist of extensive and intricate discussions of particular matters, such as kin terminology and lineage economics, but the overall argument can readily be summarised. The object of analysis is the Polynesian 'status system' and its evolution. 'Principles of status', principles that define worth, are seen, in the Polynesian case, to give 'direction to the social structure as a whole' (Goldman 1970: 5–7). The cornerstone of the argument is a classification of Polynesian societies into three categories, traditional, open and stratified:

The Traditional is essentially a religious system headed by a sacred chief and given stability by a religiously sanctioned gradation of worth. In the second system, which I call 'Open,' seniority has been modified to allow military and political effectiveness to govern status and political control. The Open system is more strongly political than religious, and stability in it must be maintained more directly by the exercise of secular powers. In the Open, status differences are no longer regularly graded but tend to be sharply defined. Finally, the third system, which I call 'Stratified,' is characterized by clearcut breaks in status that are far-reaching in their impact upon everyday life. In the Stratified system, status differences are economic and political. High ranks hold the rule and possess the land titles: the commoners are subjects and are landless.

(1970: 20)

35

The developmental process linking these stages entails shifting combinations of status and power:

In Traditional societies, status is dominant and power is subordinate; in the Open societies, power is dominant and status is subordinate; in the Stratified societies, status and power are at an approximately even level but both are more consequential than in the Traditional societies. Taking Polynesian society as a whole, it is evident that the central issue is the steady growth in power. (1970: 22)

'Status' and 'power' – glossed further as 'honour' and 'control' – therefore seem to be complementary substances, which are distinguished simply 'at a cultural level'. Their respective importance varies; neither is constituted as more fundamental (1970: 21–2).

The body of the text consists of extensive presentation of the data in terms of the attributes of the three different categories, with emphasis upon contrasts between different cases which reveal the larger progressive movement. The ordering of the examples through which these types or stages and the evolutionary process are expressed bears a problematic relationship to any actual historical developments: the society of the New Zealand Maori is set up as the original condition, yet even in simple geographic and prehistoric terms, New Zealand would have to be seen as a late and marginal extension of Polynesian society[2] (in rather the same way as some uncharitable people might see contemporary white New Zealand as a late and marginal extension of English culture).

Evolution and time

This question relates to some larger problems about the way the evolutionary process is conceived. The line taken in *Ancient Polynesian society* on this crucial point is in fact rather obscure. Goldman says that his sequence is 'hypothetical and approximate' (1970: 27). The first term suggests that what we are offered is essentially a model of social forms, perhaps divorced from their exemplifications, while the second implies that an attempt is made to reconstruct an actual sequence. Goldman maintains at one point that we cannot 'establish the precise rank order of eastern or western Polynesian societies'; that he has 'asked rather whether variations in status systems and related social structure have moved in some order of regularity from Traditional to Open and Stratified' (1970: 27). It is unclear, however, what concept of 'rank order' is rejected and how this would differ from the 'order of regularity' which is put forward as a legitimate object. He further suggests that 'the history of diffusion of Polynesian culture has no direct bearing upon the attempt to reconstruct Polynesian social evolution' because 'societies are not ordinarily caught in arrested development'; that is, the Polynesian societies on islands with longer settlement histories have undergone local change and evolution. 'Diffusion' would thus be connected with 'social evolution' via an assumption that oldest settled places have not changed since other groups moved on, and that therefore these places reflect earlier stages in the histories of more newly settled places. Such an approach is avoided because it would immediately encounter problems in Polynesia, where some of the islands with the longest settlement histories, such as Samoa and Tonga, were also those which were the most hierarchical at the time of contact. The rejection of this sort of notion permits the analysis to be free of located historical change: 'evolution' seems to take place on some distinct level. But Goldman adds that

Maori history, suggesting a branching from an early form of the Society Islands' social system, actually gives a historical foundation to the morphological view; Maori has some authenticity as an early social system. (1970: 27)

There is certainly ambiguity if not absolute contradiction here. While Maori society may have changed in various minor respects, the 'structure' is seen as an existing (in the late eighteenth- to early nineteenth-century period) manifestation of an early form. 'Arrested development' may not be mentioned, but a certain structural immobility is this argument's condition of existence: some societies reflect earlier moments in the histories of others, spatial variation reflecting temporal change. *La recherche du temps perdu* is then simply a matter of looking to another island.[3] A problem in interpreting Goldman's implicit logic arises here from the ambiguity of words such as 'divergence'. While this may be used loosely to indicate difference from a case already discussed, it strongly connotes change from some point in common. It is precisely this sort of creative confusion which allows Goldman's text to half covertly deploy concepts which have been explicitly banished. Thus the societies described not only represent a type such as 'traditional' but also provide images and reference points for the earlier histories of more advanced forms.

The ambiguity is therefore not some straightforward product of poor exposition, but rather reflects a basic shift which draws on a classically evolutionist spatialization of time (or temporalization of space), but which simultaneously frees the author from the obligation of linking this to any historical transformations. He retains the strategy of representing certain societies as archaic forms of others, but selects these on the basis of theoretical criteria rather than prehistoric depth.

The status of time in evolutionary discourse is therefore considerably more uncertain and ambiguous than one might initially have supposed. One presupposes that evolution is a temporal process, but it seems rather that the variation discussed is purely geographical. The Hawaiian system is compared with Tikopia and Easter Island societies. One sort of temporal difference is suppressed, in the sense that the sources relate to reconstructions of late eighteenth-century Hawaii, to Tikopia in 1928–29, and to nineteenth-century

Easter Island. These temporal locations are homogenized; each society as variously known is treated as an end-point of indigenous Polynesian evolutionary processes, which have generated a product independent of European movement into the area. The differences are not relevant to the construction of the argument, which rather sets up oppositions or continuities between socio-geographic referents: 'Maori', 'the new Hawaiian principle of leadership', and so on.

At another level, evolutionary argument uses a temporal metaphor to colour or valorize relationships which have no actual temporal content. This device of anthropological writing relates to the broader nature of comparative statements, which tend always to be charged or loaded in some way. If one notes that masks are used in male initiations in one place but not in another, one simply sets up a bland contrast, a marking of presence and absence. One might equally notice different house types or forms of dress. But regional contrasts almost never have this undirected, uncoloured character. 'Pre-anthropological' descriptions of native people notably construct types and systematic differences: small black pagan hill tribesmen ('bush kanakas') versus taller, lighter skinned Christian coastal groups; the civilization of the Andes versus the savagery of the Amazon – in every colonized region such differences were created or encoded. Particular attributes become resonant of more fundamental differences, such as the degree of primitiveness.

Traits or local features relate to more general differences in a similar way in more 'scientific' forms of anthropological knowledge. Variation is important because certain mechanisms or correlations are proposed which have some causal or functional effect, which is distinctly expressed or worked out in different cases. For example, I. M. Lewis has argued that spirit possession frequently provides a means for oppressed or deprived groups such as women to exert pressure upon or attack the dominant group (Lewis 1986: 23–50).[4] Once a claim of this kind has been made, either on the basis of ethnographic descriptions or theoretical expectations, further ethnographic material cannot be introduced in a neutral way. Particular facts are already charged by their relationship to prior assertions, and amount to extensions, modifications or converse illustrations. There are 'parallel instances' in Tanzania, 'analogous phenomena...among the Ba-Thonga...and Zulu'; 'the Hausa *bori* cult...is a similar though more elaborate affair' (Lewis 1986: 36–7). The argument thus has the effect of recreating the whole field of ethnographic evidence as a set of potential confirmations or disconfirmations. This applies as much to debates as to individual texts, and one body of material, such as Kachin ethnography, may be linked with a particular stance (a dynamic functionalism [Leach 1954]) or critique (Friedman's structural-Marxist challenge to ecological materialism and functionalism [1972]); other cases like 'Mead's Samoa' may have status as examples of particular gender relations. There is also the sense in which certain bodies of evidence acquire the status of 'test cases' for particular perspectives: Ian Langham has discussed the significance of the Ambrymese six-section kinship system for the Rivers–Haddon 'social organization' school from this angle (1981: 200–43).

Factual materials may therefore have very dense associations with particular arguments, but these are likely to be generally recognized: it is apparent that the distinct value of examples in a specific analysis such as Lewis's is constituted through his argument. The cases have a prior theoretical character simply because they are derived from ethnographic accounts, but they do not already have the precise charge or value which arises in particular formulations. In evolutionary discourse, on the other hand, the temporal metaphor imbues examples with value in a manner which is at once less explicit and more forceful. In Goldman's book there is no particular argument for the inclusion of such-and-such a society in the 'open' or the 'stratified' category. The classification apparently relates to unproblematic features of the groups themselves. It is thus the case that the temporal 'place' of a particular society is understood as one of its properties, rather than as something specified in an argument. The societies' hypothetical 'rank order' is merely an elaboration and articulation of a description saturated with temporal metaphors. In this case, the representation of quasi-temporal status is not usually explicit: societies are not frequently described as 'early', 'late', or 'advanced', but the writing effects such an understanding through many more particular allusions. In the stratified society of Mangareva, for example, we find institutional 'improvisations' and 'innovations'. The early vernacular traditions depict, according to Goldman, 'a traditional society well along the road to a new social order' (1970: 153, 162, 163). The former state was, of course, the traditional system, exemplified by such cases as New Zealand, which are represented almost as the absence of improvisations – just as in more general and ideological social classifications, 'primitive' societies are recognized negatively through the absences of writing, the state and money, rather than on the basis of any positive attributes.

Evolutionary movements are defined in a way which supposes certain deeply seated and largely implicit notions. The traditional society is just that – one which is structured on the whole by tradition. Rank and hierarchy are defined by a cultural order which has some arbitrary basis – in this case, birth order – which is restrictive in the sense that this ranking, rather than personal attributes, largely determines one's life and social standing. However, just like such culturally captured subjects, these ideas are not themselves free of genealogy. They can be traced back to a much broader and certainly very much cruder set of notions in European discourses about custom-bound primitives and their resistance to innovation (e.g. Thomson 1908: vii).

Although Goldman does not postulate immobility, the traditional order privileges conformity to an ascribed order, thereby circumscribing fluidity and individual rivalry.

> Legitimacy alone poses conflicting genealogical claims upon the [chiefly] title ... while legitimacy does provide an active channel for status rivalry, it seemingly has the means for controlling the consequences of status rivalry ... Genealogical disputes serve to expand the segmental organization and broaden the opportunities for rank. They do not transform the traditional system. (1970: 61)

The specifically problematic feature of the legacy of these ideas is that the movement from traditional to open is almost one from restriction to freedom. The open systems are 'loosened up', as it were: 'Power rather than rank' is the key constituent of status (1970: 85–6). Marquesan craft specialists almost embody western notions of aptitude-based social mobility: 'They had enormous prestige and good prospects for becoming wealthy and thus politically powerful' (1970: 136). Goldman saw the Marquesan system 'as the prototype of the Open society. It insists upon few givens, and leaves the field wide open for attainment' (1970: 142). The ideologically charged opposition between an ultimately constraining cultural order and the creative force of deregulated individual agency hardly requires further comment here (but cf. Thomas 1985: 224). The problem is that the force of the notion of opening up society to attainment is such that specific questions about the transformations of one system into another, which is perhaps only *incidentally* more 'fluid', are submerged. The stress upon the ordering role of 'tradition' (or specifically genealogical rank) tends to preclude serious consideration of the dynamics of systems which are never entirely encompassed by their apparently inflexible cultural orders. Equally, the emphasis on attainment and fluidity tends to erase certain forms of rigidity or structural inequality which are sometimes precisely the preconditions of 'equality of opportunity'. This is to introduce a contemporary political vocabulary, but the point is precisely that political analyses of distant peoples often play upon or are seduced by the elisions and reifications of our own meanings.

Since in the stratified system the chiefly hierarchy seems to recover and centralize the extended and developed forms of power characteristic of open societies, the whole sequence amounts to a dialectic: the opposition between the traditional and open forms is overcome in the stratified. In many scattered descriptive passages, Goldman identifies diversity – among distinct open societies, for instance – but this is somehow never systematically drawn into the model. In fact, these forays are almost suppressed. Much of the chapter on Samoa, for instance, emphasizes a distinctive development, a locally peculiar form of an open system, which seemingly had its own path somewhere away from the grand road towards the stratified system.

Differences between eastern (now American) Samoan and western Samoan patterns are noted, and it is suggested that the Manu'an pattern of rivalry was a 'more subtle version of "openness"' (1970: 245), that there was much 'dilution of the sources of access to sacred powers' (1970: 254). In introducing the discussion of Tonga, these points are set aside: Tonga 'carried forward a political evolution that in western Samoa, for example, was still incomplete' (1970: 280). Difference here is reduced to a kind of collective failure; it is as though the non-stratified systems exist *toward* the stratified system, even though the text's own discussion of Samoa points to something other. The book as a whole is almost like the political life of a city – there are all sorts of small-scale, discrete or loosely connected projects, with a peculiar or perverse thread of argument, a local claim; the whole is unevenly colonized by a larger argument, which like a mass political party covers but fails to absorb or reflect the many distinct arguments, tactics and projects of its field of activity, its object of discourse.

Museum anthropology plays evidence

The configuration of Goldman's analysis derives both from his theoretical notions and from the sources he draws upon. Any argument or analytic mode makes a range of assumptions about what can constitute 'data', about what will do and what will not. Facts may be statistics or generalizations about practice (the incidence of a form of marriage), quoted observations, or quotations from participants in the situation studied ('Women think that the pigs they rear will be theirs to eat later'). In some cases a proposition may be seen as significant in itself; in other instances, knowledge about context is demanded, but whether this context is semantic, historical or practical obviously varies. The constitution of what is acceptable as information thus encodes an argument's premises and may even incorporate aspects of what appear to be 'subsequent' interpretations. Hypotheses appear to be consequent upon an interaction of data and theory but can instead simply enunciate judgements and relationships created in the form of the evidence. I shall show that the interpretive burden of the 'raw data' of museum anthropology was in fact considerable.

An evaluation of the sources drawn into a comparative study or theory can amount to a critique simply because the weaknesses of the sources fracture the edifice 'based' upon them. One critical review of *Ancient Polynesian society* was subtitled 'Reflections on castles built of sand (and a few bits of coral)' (Howard 1972). The metaphor of argument as a building more or less securely erected on or grounded in facts which are ideally bedrock but sometimes shifting, is familiar but quite misleading in its radical separation of raw material and structure. Forms of evidence and analysis tend to be mutually implicated in an implicit and almost surreptitious way. The force of

41

Table 1. *Goldman's sources*

Island/group	Main sources
Maori	Best, Buck,[a] Firth (1929)
Manihiki/Rakahanga (Cook Is.)	Buck (1932a)[b]
Tongareva (Cook Is.)	Buck (1932b)[b]
Mangaia	Buck (1934),[b] Gill[a]
Easter Island	Métraux (1940)[d]
Marquesas	E. S. C. Handy (1923)[b]
Mangareva	Buck (1938)[b]
Society Islands	Henry (1928),[c,d] Handy, (1930)[b] Ellis (1829), Adams (1947)
Hawaii	Fornander (1878–80), Kamakau (1964), Malo (1951), Handy and Pukui (1958), a.o.
Samoa	Mead (1930),[d] Stair (1897), Turner (1884)
Tonga	Gifford (1929),[b] Martin (1827)
Uvea	Burrows (1937)[d]
Futuna	Burrows (1936)[d]
Tokelaus	Macgregor (1937)[b]
Tikopia	Firth (1936) a.o.
Pukapuka	Beaglehole and Beaglehole (1938)[b]
Niue	Loeb (1926)[d]
Ontong Java	Hogbin (1931) a.o.

a.o. = among others
[a] Several works – see Goldman for full references.
[b] Bishop Museum research published by the Bishop Museum.
[c] Henry's work is an exceptional case in that it was compiled from some of the papers of her grandfather, the missionary J. M. Orsmond, who was active in the Society Islands from 1818 to 1856.
[d] Research by temporary associate of the Bishop Museum, but published by the Museum and therefore reflecting the standard form of the Bulletins.

argument arises frequently from unexamined metaphors, rather than from overt claims.

Evidence and argument seem especially to be each other's shadows in Goldman's book, which draws on a distinct and restricted range of sources. Although stray references are made to the publications of early voyagers such as Cook and de Bougainville, to missionary memoirs and 'beachcomber' books like William Mariner's *Tonga Islands*, the accounts of particular islands and island groups depend heavily upon the ethnographic bulletins of the Bishop Museum (see table 1).[5]

Ethnographic totalization and the erasure of history

Museum anthropology was an enterprise conducted by institutions which were usually at least as concerned with natural history. The setting of the work, and the fact that practitioners were often initially trained in natural science subjects, made for some equation between native cultures and other phenomena studied by museums. These exist as assemblages of elements distributed across space which are to be observed, recorded, and, if possible, collected by competent researchers. Artifacts, plants and fossils are, of course, objects rather than agents: the traits and elements of a culture are likewise the primary things to be known. It may be the case that natives have been actively engaged in the creation of an ethnographic depiction of their society, but this is an uncomplicated process which feeds into the procedure of trained description.

Ethnographic phenomena are classified in a sort of grid which is seen to cover the totality, but is not thought of as a problematic or theoretically-laden set of categories which come to constitute the 'data'. Rather it is simply a set of headings under which material (naturally) falls. There is in fact some continuity between museum work on natural phenomena and ethnology, since archaeology and material culture studies dealt with inanimate objects such as houses, boats and stone remains which might fall into manifestly discrete functional or morphological classes. Since physical anthropology or anthropometry was also an area of endeavour, ethnology proper would certainly have been the odd subject out if the approach of objectified classification had not been extended into social and cultural domains. The substantial number of broadly ethnographic Bishop Museum bulletins therefore organise information into short sections and subsections under a roughly standardised pattern of headings: Introduction (with a very brief account of the circumstances of field research); Geography (basic information on island size, climate, etc., and often impressionistic statements about the abundance or otherwise of a particular island's or group's resources); European contact (usually dealt with very briefly); Traditional history (sometimes presented in considerable genealogical and mythical detail, depending on the adequacy of the material); followed by accounts of many more specific matters – 'Social Organization', 'Titles', 'Rank', 'Religion', 'The Priesthood', 'Warfare', 'Individual in Society', subdivided under 'Birth', 'Infancy', 'Puberty', and so on (sometimes 'Marriage' would be dealt with in this context, sometimes under 'Kinship' or 'The Family'). In some cases, much of a report might be devoted to various elements of material culture, but in cases of larger islands or island groups, this was usually published separately. The specific ordering of sections varied, but in any instance matters which others might think to be closely linked, such as

'Chiefs' and 'Regalia' or 'Ritual' are found to be segregated under larger headings such as 'Social Organization' and 'Religion' (e.g. Buck 1934).

The classificatory approach did not, of course, permit space for the analysis or interpretation of social relations as a total system or social dynamics. Thus general statements might be made in passing about such matters as the importance of warfare in the pursuit of prestige, but systemic links were not elaborated upon: the general view is conveyed in occasional impressionistic passages, while connections between warfare and production, and the importance of control over land, or the identifications between warrier-chiefs and mythical figures are, for example, very much cut about and buried. And while a certain, rather superficial comparison of institutions between different islands is facilitated, a sense of the differences between larger systems is most difficult to derive from the bulletins. This stems partly from a resistance even to a rudimentary holism, which is manifested in Buck's almost sarcastic comparison between functionalism and what he described as the Museum's 'historical method'. He evidently thought that the functional method involved the 'limiting of inquiry into the case histories of individual lives' and 'ignoring the bondage of the historical past'. While the latter point was justified, the former implies a complete lack of familiarity with the literature. Apparently with *The sexual life of savages* in mind, he noted censoriously that 'more importance appears to be attached to the intimate details of the technique of coitus and its various postures than to the technical details involved in the construction of a canoe and making it move' (1945: 127). The uncompromising empiricism and ignorance of functional theory betrayed here was probably shared by the other museum ethnologists, but some of the outsiders like Mead and Métraux who wrote bulletins on the basis of temporary museum fellowships had more up-to-date views; Burrows, for instance, was interested in the conjunction of internal processes and environmental factors in the process of 'cultural differentiation' (1939; cf. Kirch 1984: 9–10). But the more explicitly analytical work of these writers tended to be developed later, outside the framework of museum publication; in the bulletins themselves the descriptive endeavour was certainly seen in all cases as an untheoretical exercise. The project of ethnology was not to be reduced to some partial or motivated interpretation, grounded in a set of intellectual interests, but rather entailed a total appropriation in knowledge of the object: the task was to capture and authoritatively depict the cultures of a group of islands.[6]

The objective of work was 'a complete survey of the Polynesian people' (Buck 1945: 50). The aim was, however, qualified: 'to gain a picture of native culture as it existed before the changes due to foreign contact began to take place' (*ibid*: 125). Although the importance of studying what was called 'acculturation' was acknowledged, there was an insistence upon the prior need to know the aboriginal system in its pure form: 'in the study of a

44

vanishing culture, a picture of what the culture was is required before it can be determined what has vanished and what remains' (1945: 126). This statement reflects an extremely simple notion of what culture contact and colonial confrontations have meant. What is native is simply in a process of fading away. It may be less visible, but it has not apparently changed through accommodation, reaction or adaptation to new conditions, nor does transformation seem to consist of anything more than displacement. Indigenous culture exists in a quantity which is reduced more or less according to the degree of foreign influence, so that by a certain date there may be 'a little' or 'very little' left to observe (e.g. E. S. C. Handy 1923: 4–5; Thompson 1940: 5; cf. Goldman's usage, 1970: 126, 319, 329, 379–80, 396).[7] This notion is especially understandable in eastern Polynesia, where depopulation and colonial strategies among other factors did have a shattering impact on indigenous institutions. However, the fading of presence into absence implies a highly restricted and unsatisfactory conception of change, even if a certain historical period saw some institutions or customs abandoned or forgotten. Another metaphor of Buck's suggests a somewhat different idea:

At the late period of a recent study, however, the true native picture had been obscured by the accretions of over a century of contact with a foreign culture. Here again, the historical method [i.e. the study of myths, genealogies and legends] was useful in clearing off the layers which covered the stone age stratum beneath.

(Buck, 1945: 126)

In this formula practices such as Christian marriage are additions which can be subtracted from the untruth to produce the truth. Goldman expresses a distinct variant of this notion when he notes that, despite the ravages of European contact on the populations of Uvea and the Tokelaus, 'domestic or household culture' could still be observed and recorded (1970: 319, 341). This is to suppose that because families, as opposed to non-Christian rituals, for example, still existed, these were an untransformed remnant of early culture. In fact, the activities of missions and colonial processes have led to transformations of gender relations and domestic groups across the Pacific (Jolly and Macintyre 1988; Thomas 1987).

There is in all these conceptions an overall dichotomy between 'native culture' which has a unitary existence and the various effects of foreign contact. The complete disconnection is brought out at one point in Burrows's *Ethnology of Uvea*, which incorporates most of a traditional narrative compiled by a Catholic priest.[8] The latter part of the text is, however, not reproduced, because it 'treats of recent foreign contacts, mainly European, and throws no light on Uvean culture' (1937: 40). These matters seem remarkably clear cut!

Although pure native culture is apparently understood as what existed

45

before contact, the point of this definition is not historical specificity but simply the absence of foreign contamination. Social relations in the Society Islands in the 1760s (just before the islanders were encountered by Captain Wallis and his 'outriggerless canoe' as the ship, the *Dolphin*, was perceived) are of no particular interest in themselves. The 'native culture' prior to contact is thus an amorphous and atemporal category, quite unlike 'Tahiti in the 1970s' or 'Augustan Rome'. Nor is there ever any attempt to reconstruct the political affairs – particular conflicts, individuals' and lineages' situations and strategies – of a certain time, although such information might fill out through specificity and ground in practice a more general depiction of the 'native culture'. But the crucial feature of this 'native culture' is, of course, neither temporal nor spatial location but authenticity (cf. Clifford 1988: 232).

The extent to which Buck regarded the exercise as having been successfully completed by 1945 is quite remarkable:

The field survey of Polynesia has been practically completed. Expeditions under the auspices of Bishop Museum have done field work in every island group except Easter Island, Niue, Chatham Island, New Zealand, and the Ellice Islands. Easter Island, Niue, and Chatham Island were visited by trained anthropologists from other institutions, but Bishop Museum published the results of their field work. New Zealand was left to her own capable students. Of the Ellice Islands, the atolls of Funafuti and Vaitupu have been studied by capable men, but the other atolls in the group may provide additional material to round off the picture. Thus, for Polynesia proper, it may be said that the only group now worth a field expedition is the Ellice Islands. This statement is not meant as a deterrent to people with private means who may wish to follow up some special project in the field, particularly in acculturation and psycho-anthropology.

Bishop Museum publications of the field studies have practically covered every phase of anthropology in history, legends, material culture, social organization, religion, and physical anthropology. Though the information may be thin in parts, such weaknesses are not due to the authors but to the fact that the native informants could not supply what they did not have. The information supplied by present-day informants was supplemented by earlier information contained in old native manuscripts, and the published literature was carefully combed for additional information. Thus, the data on each island group has been brought up-to-date and will save students the tiresome task of searching through other works which may not be available to them. Though I may be suspected of bias, I consider that the regional survey of Polynesia has been well done and that Bishop Museum publications may be regarded as the authoritative works on this area. (1945: 123–4)

An 'authoritative' work makes a claim to power, and there are many points at which Buck implicitly asserts the Museum's monopoly over the knowing of Polynesia. Great value is attached to any work done specifically by Bishop Museum staff. The work of other researchers on places such as Easter Island which the Museum saw fit to publish is evidently almost of the same calibre. The possibility that these studies are less than definitive is excluded. The only further projects countenanced are those on particular topics such as 'acculturation', but these are of such a trivial nature that 'people with private means' are those who might like to pursue them – presumably Buck thought that research funds might be better directed elsewhere. He indicates that not only are field projects complete but that 'the published literature' was searched for further information, and that students no longer need waste time searching for dusty volumes.[9]

It is usually freely acknowledged by the authors of the ethnographic bulletins that oral memories, observed behaviour and published information are all drawn into the report. While early voyagers' narratives may be quoted, whole traditional histories reproduced, and individual informants at times acknowledged, there are many passages where sources are entirely obscure. In some accounts of marriage and kinship, for example, the past tense is used generally but not exclusively, and one cannot tell whether particular practices were observed or were no longer to be observed at the time of fieldwork; if the latter, one does not know if the report derived from a local account of what things were like ten years ago, or from a navigator's observations of the 1840s (e.g. Macgregor 1937: 40f.).

The detemporalized product cannot therefore be considered as authoritative as Buck would wish, especially when the brevity of periods of field research is considered. Buck's seventeen days on Tongareva stand out as an insecure basis for an ethnographic report – particularly for one supposedly encapsulating the truth of the place, obviating the possibility of any further useful work – but even those who spent longer in the field were rarely there for more than seven or eight months. The broad experience of some of the researchers in Polynesia would have meant that they probably learnt languages very quickly and made much more of a short period than any apprentice researcher could.[10]

Field research methods, as much as the mere brevity of periods of research, hardly diminish one's reservations about the adequacy of some information collected. In many cases techniques are not discussed or are mentioned very briefly, but Buck gave an account of his own main procedure:

The plan I have tried to follow during field expeditions is to call, or sit in at, a meeting of the people and explain to them that the object of inquiry is to put their history, traditions, crafts and customs on record for the outside world to appreciate. The collecting of information becomes a community project, which the people strive to make as complete as possible. They will indicate the best informants, or the best informants will indicate themselves. (1945: 32)

The objective is thus a synthesized corpus, as though there was one correct account of traditional history and customs. The differences between informants relate to quality, to more or less perfect knowledge, rather than to perspective. But in some Polynesian societies chiefly perceptions of society were certainly not shared by the entire group. There is no effort to sort out or analyse different viewpoints. In many parts of Polynesia certain groups –

47

often those located around the best anchorages – acquired a degree of dominance because they interacted more with Europeans than people on other parts of an island, or people on other islands within a group. This sort of centralization, or reorientation of asymmetries, was, of course, a very general feature of colonial change. Buck's synthetic approach is likely also to reflect the perceptions from such central or newly central places, rather than those from other localities. In a western political context this would not merely be like adding together the perspectives of the Conservative and Labour parties to produce a picture of a total British political culture, since it was as though this was done in one constituency which happened to be that of the Prime Minister.[11]

Possible entanglements with histories of local asymmetry and uneven colonialism had prior effects on the context of fieldwork, but at least Buck's own work was also intimately enmeshed in the continuing intervention of administration in the local scene, as is apparent from his account of his Mangaian research:

As a return for the assistance of the Cook Islands Administration, I agreed to act in the place of the Resident Agent...during his absence on leave...

Except for morning sick parades, the weekly court, which occupied less than an hour, and the monthly paying of civil servants, my official duties made little demand on my time. In my official position I was authorized to use the resources of the government in such a way as I deemed expedient. The government, therefore, devoted its attention to the ethnological survey. The police in the villages acted as assistants in gathering the people together for the purpose of making head and body measurements. The district and subdistrict chiefs were called upon to conduct official visits of inspection through their districts. The maraes and old battlefields were visited and described by local experts...   (Buck 1934: 3)

On Tongareva he evidently also gained considerable information through attending land court sittings. Given that information was derived through public channels rather than confidential interviews, the facts could only reflect the interests and tactics of particular parties. (Someone such as Buck who was clearly identified as a friend of certain colonial officials might well have been unable to get different information through private discussions in any event.) The sum of various motivated accounts is not some 'whole truth' but simply a blurred image abstracted from the circumstances of its production. As feminist critiques have pointed out, the same problem arises for more recent ethnographic studies of gender relations if it is presupposed that culture is above all a shared system of meanings; this view can only suppress competing male and female views. If the object is the 'native culture' in some generalised sense, there is little room for situational variation or contested definitions: vocalized dissent becomes 'noise' in the statisticians' sense of irrelevant complexity. Historical and anthropological accounts which implicitly suppose that there is a homogenous culture are, unfortunately, likely to provide support for the elites who manipulate such ideologies. That, of course, is very convenient for researchers who have no desire to offend those who control the colonial or post-colonial country being studied, but is often consistent neither with respectable politics nor good anthropology.

Goldman offered an evolutionary argument which, despite some irrelevant and misleading qualifications, reproduced the classic evolutionary view of social diversity: simpler or less stratified societies are regarded as the antecedents of more complex and hierarchical systems. Geographical and historical difference are erased in abstract time, in a master narrative which is at once linear and progressive. A particular evolutionary story may refrain from declaring its place in the overall mythic image of the step-by-step advancement of humanity – a story which distances 'them' from 'us', and justifies 'their' subordination to 'us' – but the particular tract nevertheless expresses the ideology in general, and does something to sustain it.

The evolutionary master narrative also imposes something particular upon the societies it encompasses. It represents them in certain terms, making them similar to the extent that they seem to be related, yet different enough to express some transformation or movement from one to the other. This difference or transformation is not, of course, unmarked variation, mere dissimilarity, but carries always a directional value. Any difference is thus either positively or negatively charged: the form of an institution is always more advanced or developed in one case than another, and thus represents the 'growth' of something which already exists in an inchoate or primitive form in the 'earlier' (but in reality contemporaneous) society.

There are a number of ways in which evidence is organized so as to facilitate this kind of construction. These do not necessarily derive from a particular effort to distort ethnographic knowledge in a way consistent with an evolutionary argument, but rather emerge as a result of some specific methods as well as from certain overall features of anthropological discourse. In the case of museum work, it is clear that total insensitivity towards historical factors produces a blurred and generalized depiction of indigenous social forms and customs. This was exacerbated by the tendency to neglect variation in space, within island groups and communities. Most museum-based projects tended to deal with regions, with Siberia or the whole of Polynesia, and it is therefore likely that the similarities between societies across the region will be exaggerated. Investigators will fill in their scanty knowledge of certain localities (which might have been visited briefly) on the basis of better-known and often hegemonic or central places. There are thus a variety of tendencies toward homogenization, both within accounts of particular societies, and within the broader regional group which is being appropriated within knowledge. Ethnographic data drawn together from a

49

diffusionist perspective can thus seem dedicated to an evolutionary synthesis. The ways in which this leads to misconstruction in a particular case are explored in the next chapter. It is worth emphasizing, though, that the tendency to 'homogenize' culture has not been superseded, and is almost certainly more developed in modern anthropological discourse than in the museum studies I have discussed. If the overall movement of analysis is a systematizing one toward generalities, toward the underlying principles or basic properties – whether social or cultural – of a system, then local variation, historic idiosyncracy, and verbalized or silent dissent can only subtract from the work of interpretation. 'Ethnology' may have been displaced by 'anthropology', but in each case the orientation of the discourse has concealed the actual process of history, but implicitly sustained the larger chronological scheme of evolution.

5

Untying evidence, rethinking transformations

The notions behind museum ethnography have a general impact on subsequent syntheses and analyses. The dissociation of 'native culture' from recent historical change leads, in Goldman's book for instance, to a restricted and somewhat abstract notion of longer-term evolution which excludes the short-term dynamics arising from European contact. The latter occupy the domains of 'social change' and 'acculturation' which cannot speak to longer-term histories.

There are also more specific connections between the constitution of particular ahistorical descriptions and elements of interpretation. Interpretations are partly implicit in what becomes 'data', which is seen as external to argument, and partly also overt in texts such as Goldman's which are more explicitly analytical exercises. The links are hidden from readers because it is pretended that a particular text is simply a 'source' which may contain omissions or even errors but is not laced with interpretation.

These issues are explored through a re-examination of the so-called 'open' societies, and particularly the cases of Easter Island and the Marquesas Islands. Ideas are identified in E. S. C. Handy's Bishop Museum publication which re-emerge in Goldman's account, facilitating a particular evolutionary argument. Handy's views can be questioned on the basis of early descriptions of particular social relations, which provide the basis for a different model of Marquesan society. In conjunction with reinterpretations of political relations and prehistories of other islands, this leads to quite a different argument about the 'evolutionary' situation of at least some of the 'open' societies.

The case of *The native culture in the Marquesas*

The Bishop Museum research on the Marquesas provides an appropriate test case, since E. S. C. Handy's ethnographic report could hardly be considered one of the Museum's slighter publications. Handy was in the Marquesas[1] for nine months, from September 1920 to June 1921, with Ralph Linton, who studied the archaeology and material culture (Linton 1923, 1925) and his

51

wife, Willowdean Chatterton Handy, who was described as a 'volunteer associate', that is, an unpaid researcher. She subsequently published studies of art and tattooing (1923, 1938) and, much later, an informative popular account of the Marquesas at the time of the expedition (1965). The period of field research was thus one of the longest upon which any Bishop Museum bulletin was based and in fact drew on the efforts of three fieldworkers, as well as some exceptionally detailed missionary manuscripts.[2]

Handy's overall image of tribal Marquesan society was of a relatively egalitarian system which was 'fluid' in the sense that it permitted ambitious individuals to secure privileged positions. A contrast with more stratified Polynesian societies such as Hawaii and Tahiti which looked more like kingdoms and appeared to have possessed more rigid rank structures was implied. Handy recognized that there was some evidence for a more hierarchical structure in parts of the group, but attributed this to a distinct migration – a reflection of a Boasian, diffusionist perspective, which for the most part was submerged by intricate descriptive ethnography.

Certain emphases in Handy's image of Marquesan society seem to reflect a disagreement with French writers such as the missionary Delmas who saw greater inequality in the old indigenous systems, which had been substantially transformed by the time of Handy's research. Divergent interpretations of the nature of hierarchy reveal underlying links between source materials, methods and arguments, as I attempt to show in this section.

Handy reacted particularly against the indiscriminate use of the word 'king' in some accounts of Marquesan life, and stressed that chiefly authority was limited. He claimed that the reports of some early observers brought 'out clearly the communism and simple democratic nature of the tribe' (1923: 35).[3] The impression of a Russian visitor, Krusenstern, was that should a chief 'venture to strike anyone, he would infallibly meet with like return' (Krusenstern 1813: 165, quoted in Handy 1923: 35). This observation about behaviour or expected behaviour hardly bears upon larger patterns of respect, authority, or dependence. Unless one saw the capacity to hit subjects with impunity as a standard chiefly prerogative, the point has little significance, since there are in many societies people with certain kinds of power or authority (such as European judges) who would 'meet with like return' or at least public censure if they assaulted others. But there seems to be an uncomplicated notion that power is manifested in various ways which require no contextual specification. Something like the capacity to deploy violence is simply an indicator which can be observed in various cases and is automatically significant.

It also seems to be assumed that 'a chief' should be expected to have some sort of obvious control or authority over all the people of a place. This is consistent with anthropological constructs of chiefs and, in fact, with what is more typical in Oceania. The crucial feature of chieftainship was in general the chief's ritual work, which alone was the fundamental cause of agricultural production, successful fishing, and well-being in general. This created a generalized asymmetry and dependence, which was manifested in a steady stream of offerings to the chief, most of which tended to be redistributed. The chief was thus focal and encompassing both in society's self-image and in practice – or at least in movements of food, which were virtually the substance of social relations across Oceania. Because this situation was both more typical, and probably also reflected an ancient common pattern, it is desirable to evaluate the divergence of specific societies from whatever may be constructed as a hypothetical ancestral system. But whether or not a particular case of chieftainship corresponds to one's expectations (on the basis of what is typical of the region) has little necessarily to do with the strength or weakness of political power. Handy's assumption seems to have been that because chiefs did not appear to have as much behavioural control as was typical elsewhere, there was less inequality or stratification in the whole system. But this was a *non sequitur* precisely because the Marquesan system was different: the chief did not have the privileged ritual situation, did not mediate between the people in general and the principal deities, and there was therefore no basis for an encompassing, paternalistic chieftainship. Resources were, however, unequally distributed, and the most important asymmetrical social relations existed between prominent individuals (of both sexes), who were often not chiefs, and their followers, who frequently depended on a 'great' man or woman for access to land.[4]

To further support the thesis that power was restricted, Handy also quoted a writer he called 'an early missionary visitor' who wrote that 'They could hardly be said to have the rudest systems of civil government. They had a sort of democracy of liberty, or license, without law' (J. Alexander 1895: 223, in Handy 1923: 35–6). This writer had not in fact been to the Marquesas, but was drawing on the accounts of earlier missionaries who had attempted to establish a mission on Nukuhiva in 1833 and 1834 (C. Alexander 1934). More importantly, the context and motivation of this statement are neglected. The total failure of some evangelical missions to gain any influence was to some extent explained away at the time by the lack of coherent Marquesan authority; the later, popular publication produced not only a cruder image, but one which reflected a wider discourse in which certain Pacific societies were characterised as disordered and anarchic. Various writers suggested that the Marquesans had 'no laws', 'no religion', 'no marriage' and even 'no regular meals' (Troost 1829: 225; Hale 1845: 7–8; Armstrong 1838; Ryazanov 1825: 86; Fleurieu 1801, I: 110; Shillibeer 1817: 45). It is striking that Hawaiian teachers writing about the Marquesans, and a Scottish Presbyterian referring to Aneityum in southern Vanuatu, could use almost the same words (from Judges 21: 25) in lamenting the uncomfortable lack of authority: 'Every one does what is right in his own mind' (Kekela 1854: 26, cf. J. Inglis, quoted by Spriggs 1981: 59). All these accounts arose from situations in which islanders were unwilling to co-operate with foreigners who were making specific attempts to alter indigenous arrangements or practices. (Visitors in ships such as Bougainville who had no desire to change the native system rather celebrated the apparent lack of behavioural regulation.) In other contexts Europeans have supposed that certain natives possessed an innate repugnance for work, without perhaps noting that the work which was specifically unwelcome was that to be done for foreigners on unfavourable terms. The formation of these representations is interesting, partly because they effectively denied legitimacy to any indigenous political order, and justified the efforts of missionaries and colonial authorities to reorganize relations – but such depictions could hardly be credited with any sort of accuracy. The point is a simple one of historical method: statements must be considered in their contexts, and are frequently revealing about the situational interests of speakers, rather than whatever is being judged or remarked upon. In the Pacific context, this requires a detailed analysis of what particular writers and observers were doing in the islands. It is not enough simply to read their material, without looking at the success or failure of their projects, and the operations their texts performed in relation to contextualization, rationalization, legitimation and advertisement.

Bishop Museum writers were often critical of missionary 'bias' (e.g. Buck 1945: 27–9) – which expressed a unidimensional view of the discursive properties of these sets of representations of indigenous life – but their own use of mission sources drew precisely on the elements of such texts which were most circumscribed by European preoccupations. Any descriptions belonging to a western anthropology, or to the traditions of observation which are that discipline's precursors, must, of course, be in English or some other European language, and will embody a western logic in various ways. However, the extent to which this logic saturates a text and deprives it of any depictive significance is variable. It is thus misleading to regard some statements as 'biased' in a simple way and others as free of such taint. A description of a particular transaction is highly likely to entail a western model of agency, individual motivation and effect; such categories can be scrutinized in anthropological or philosophical analysis, and it can be taken for granted that they permeate all western representations in a more or less complex way. There would thus be no sense in rejecting an account because it was 'ethnocentric' in these terms, since no representation can or should constitute itself in a conceptual vacuum. Particular forms of criticism can single out aspects of the ideology which animates a particular text for scrutiny, and this exercise must always be linked to intellectual interests which have their own undiscussed tenets.[5] The problem is thus not 'bias' or ethnocentrism in general, but the fact that specific kinds of discussion in western discourse do reveal far less about whatever is ostensibly being described than the concerns and perceptions of the observer and writer. General expositions of 'the native type' or 'national character' are of this kind, and can hardly avoid a distinct and dubious imputation of pseudo-psychological propensities and dark reflections of otherness. That is, the divergence between the people described and some 'us' entirely distorts the actual character of the 'others'. Handy's uncritical use of motivated syntheses such as Alexander's book mentioned above thus courts fallacies which a reading of more casual accounts of events might avoid.

The poorly-specified limits of chiefly power were, for Handy, aspects of a loose or fluid social system. Despite a tendency for privileged positions to be inherited, 'there was nothing to prevent any man or woman in the tribe from rising to the highest positions, those of chief and inspirational priest' (1923: 36–7). In so far as it applied to *tau'a*, inspired priests, this statement is correct and almost tautological, because they were shamanic figures whose power related precisely to the fact that they were chosen by the deities, irrespective of prior social status. Choice took place suddenly, and was manifested by ecstatic possession and wild fits; this was, of course, arbitrary from the viewpoint of social structure or any larger hierarchical principle.

However, all the problems of the Museum's method of ahistorical distillation are crystallised in this assertion about chiefs, which neglects the great impact of contact and many sorts of violence in the course of the nineteenth century (see Dening 1980). Handy was aware, of course, that the positions of chiefs had been dramatically eroded; it is unlikely that anyone used or attached any weight to the chiefly title at the time of his fieldwork. The problem is rather that he must have assumed that informants' statements about the nature of the system in the past referred to a period before chieftainship declined, rather than some later date (just as Radcliffe-Brown assumed that the statements of Andamanese informants about the past related to the period before the 1858 occupation). But the nature of chiefly power began to change very soon after the early contacts with European voyagers in the late eighteenth century, and the institution seems to have been dramatically weakened after 1842, when the French annexation of the group led to conflict at Vaitahu and Taiohae, where garrisons were stationed, and where rebellions of sorts were put down. Although this was certainly an irregular process, which did not affect other areas until later, there is a striking contrast between the vigorous rivalry and expansionism of chiefs in the 1830s, and the weakness of their successors.[6]

But the principal memories of even the parents of Handy's informants would relate to a later period, such as from the 1860s on, when local groups seem to have been acutely fractured and traditional leaders at least half displaced by Catholic priests, gendarmes and other officials, and settlers. In so far as it persisted, chieftainship was shaped by intervention: influential

Europeans sometimes decided who should be chief, and there are a number of reports of people of servile status assuming the office, which seems to have been unheard of earlier.

The informants' statements upon which Handy's claim was based are highly likely to relate to late cases such as these. There is no reason why informants should have distinguished the situation between 1860 and 1890 from the period sixty to one hundred years earlier; given that there had been a continuous process of change, and that a society free of foreigners really was in the remote past, it is unlikely that there was any indigenous periodization of nineteenth-century history which particular circumstances or changes might have been linked to.[7] Elsewhere Handy speaks of a 'great war' on Fatuiva as though it belonged in some distant, pre-European past (1923: 30), but it is quite clear from the events mentioned that the conflict was one witnessed and documented by Hawaiian teachers from 1856 on. Because the notion of the 'native culture' excludes post-contact events, that is the indigenous history which is also a European history, there is somehow no space between the past time of the living 'native culture' and the time of professional observation. There is, of course, a temporal gap, but what has taken place in that is either subtraction or addition. Things like myths and rituals have been forgotten, and western clothes or ideas may be adopted, but there has been no creative reworking or dynamic accommodation. If there is a memory at all it must, therefore, pertain to the 'native culture'. But it is all too apparent that some of these 'traditional memories' either relate to events of the colonial period or reflect some positive rendering of the past consistent with the difficult and tragic circumstances of that period.[8]

Early Marquesan society: an alternate view

The errors here arise from a failure to recognize the extent to which Marquesan society had in fact departed from a Polynesian pattern of hierarchical solidarity in which chieftainship encompassed society and was central to it. Marquesan chiefs had no ritual centrality with respect to prosperity and production and likewise no generalized titular ownership of land. The readers of documents encounter a series of general statements which suggest that there was no higher-level chiefly ownership which might have been reflected in tribute or prestations as Handy suggested, and moreover that there were autonomous landholders who held their own tracts quite independently. The relationship Handy described, in which services and a portion of the product were exchanged for rights to use land, certainly existed, but between landholders – including chiefs – and their dependants, rather than between chiefs and others allotted land by chiefs.[9] He mistook references to such relations between chiefs and people for the overall form of the system, and completely overlooked the non-chiefly landowners, whose position might be compared to that of Tahitian *ra'atira*, if William Ellis's account of the situation of that class was correct: they 'held their land, not from the gift of the King, but from their ancestors' (1829, II: 343–4). It is, however, only the range of evidence about particular relations and the events through which they were worked out which enables one to make a sensible choice between general descriptive propositions of this kind, and to see beyond them to a sense of the system in practice.

Marquesan economic inequalities were incorporated into but not generated by a caste-like hierarchy of *tapu* grades. The overall opposition was between male and female and was crucially worked out through rules that women could not eat with men in their *tapu* eating houses, or eat food destined for men, while men could partake of food belonging to women if they wished (although there were many more specific restrictions applying to certain foods and times). This gender opposition was cut across by rank differences among both women and men; some high grades amounted to elite clubs, while others connected with particular occupations were sometimes more broadly based. *Tapu* and *me'ie* (free of *tapu*) were contextual, depending on the status of the other party at a particular time. Grades were usually distinguished by particular facial tattoos and usually by a special eating house. The hierarchy readily incorporated groups with claims to status but lacking a place in the genealogical hierarchy: thus there seems to have been warrior grades, and a grade composed of people distinguished by their property, but otherwise common (Crook 1800: 118). This unitary hierarchy ordered by basic oppositions was a distinctive Marquesan development. It seems to have broken down early in the nineteenth century – apparently existing only in a reduced form even in the 1830s – and escaped Handy's attention altogether.

While Marquesan chiefs were prominent and powerful figures, they were not really central to Marquesan social life: a distinct, complicated hierarchy, not connected with the chiefly line, had developed. Chieftainship was disconnected from shamanism, which controlled the fundamental, life-giving ritual capacities, as well as from any larger encompassing field of asymmetrical relations connected with the control of key resources: the privileged positions had become generalized among landholders.

The simple notion in Handy's account that the chief was like a father to the whole tribe is certainly wide of the mark. At the same time, he fails to recognize various distinct aspects of hierarchy, and diminishes the overall degree of inequality. The situation of apparent flexibility is curiously equated with relative equality – presumably manifesting the liberal and primarily American notion of equality as competitive equality of opportunity. Handy in fact notes that while early writers from monarchical Europe tended to see kings in mere chiefs, visitors from the United States such as the missionary C. S. Stewart and Captain David Porter had a clearer vision: the former even

57

referred to the Marquesas as a 'republic *en sauvage*'. In suggesting that these authors recognized the fundamentally egalitarian character of Marquesan society because they came from republican America, Handy posits an identity between the sorts of egalitarianism which exist in the two places. If these were instead fundamentally different, the Americans would not have been better equipped to perceive the society. It would be uncharitable to suggest that Handy took this equation too seriously, but in the context of his discussion it does imply a more general conflation of ascribed rank and inequality on one side, and competition and equality on the other (cf. Jolly 1987). This notion is objectionable because it reflects an uncritical adoption and projection of the values of capitalism, but also happens to be totally misleading in so far as it is applied to Polynesian societies. Marquesan property relations were fluid, and were not defined by any caste-like system of ascribed rank, but were certainly unequal, while various ascribed distinctions did not generate relations of exploitation or dependency in practice.

The point here is not simply that the deeper concepts and methods of museum anthropology generate Handy's particular misrepresentations. More significantly, as Handy's account becomes Goldman's raw material, these turn to facilitate a particular evolutionary understanding.

The initial fault is that Marquesan society is placed on a sort of scale from less authoritarian (or politically hierarchical, or centralized) to more so (or more stratified). I lump a set of distinct terms together to underline the vagueness which a unilineal view of political development imposes. A variety of distinct circumstances, political capacities, social relations, and behaviours are compressed onto one axis. The ability of a leader to use violence thus becomes a sign of the same thing as, say, the control over land or ritual privilege. Less of whatever this is means that we witness primitive communism or primitive democracy; more of these signs of power mean a kind of feudalism or 'rigidity'. This coalescence of an array of asymmetries and images has not, unfortunately, been expunged from modern anthropology, which is supposedly very careful in refraining from imposing inappropriate western categories upon other cultures: Lederman (1986), for instance, sees the Mendi as living in a sort of small-scale democracy.

Because Marquesan society obviously lacked some of the criteria of a more unequal or centralized system, it has effectively been located on the egalitarian end of this compelling spectrum. The central metaphor is one of individual flexibility or fluidity, as opposed to regulation and authority. Certain observations of apparent anarchy are thus seized upon, and translated into the 'fluidity' of the Marquesan system; between *The native culture* and *Ancient Polynesian society* the divergence of Marquesan society from something more typically Polynesian is reduced to movement from relative rigidity to fluidity. Despite this shift the chief is seen to maintain centrality and allot land in the more stratified Marquesan societies. There is thus some sort of loosening-up, but no actual structural transformation. Structural transformations are in fact invisible unless they map onto the unilineal path from more to less stratified. The ambiguous position of Marquesan society – looser yet still centralized – is crucial because the Marquesas seem to be on Goldman's path from 'open' to 'stratified'; this particular instance makes the movement from one form to the other plausible. The 'example', the 'data', which appear to be quite independent of Goldman's theorizing, are thus already fashioned in quite a particular way; the case is already situated in relation to the more stratified Polynesian societies, and although Handy had no particular evolutionary bent, his unidimensional view of power and hierarchy was consistent with the paths of social development which Goldman proceeded to map out. 'Paths' is perhaps the wrong word, since the exercise was directed not at a plurality of meandering routes, expressing the diverse purposes of people who, say, used a forest, but sought instead to define a necessary road which climbed from one condition to the next. An image less easy to reconcile with the diverse social projects of real people, or the complicated histories of real groups, which follow contours as often as they go up or down. In any case, the evidence can be perceived differently, and if the transformation and singular erosion of Marquesan chieftainship is recognized, this society's significance in a larger historical scheme becomes much more problematic.

From distinction to transgression: the evolution of 'open' societies

I have suggested that Marquesan society was misrepresented in both Goldman's sources and in his interpretation. Some anthropologists ignore longer-term change, or argue that an evolutionary framework should be totally rejected. So far as Pacific societies are concerned, I suggest that an understanding of longer-term history is crucial. A comparative discussion of east Polynesian societies can perhaps illustrate some of the social transformations which took place in the region. These cases show that specific ethnographic features can be analysed in various ways, but not actually explained, without reference to a longer pattern of change and development. A view of eastern Pacific social 'evolution' is developed which is very different to that of Goldman, yet insists on the importance of the contextualization of local relations in the histories which differentiated one locality from another.

On Easter Island, now known as Rapanui among its inhabitants, the 'king' or high chief (*ariki mau*), who came from the Miru clan, was said to be sacred and possess great prestige. Like Marquesan chiefs he was surrounded by *tapu* which extended to his personal property and food. His head was so sacred

59

that his hair could never be cut, and any article he used subsequently became *tapu* (Métraux 1940).

A chant recorded by Métraux makes it clear that the notional basis of this status was the influence of the *ariki mau* over nature:

> What does the king make fertile in the country?
> The yams, the taro, the sweet potatoes the king makes grow in the country.
> Now he makes the yams, the sweet potatoes, the sugar cane, the shoots favourable in the country, in the shade.
> What does the king make fertile in the country?
> The turtle, its abdominal shell, its legs – these he makes grow in the country.   (Métraux 1940: 133–4)

The formula is repeated in relation to various fish, ferns, plants, natural elements, and so forth. For one of Métraux's informants, the relationship between the *ariki mau* and fertility was illustrated by the fact that the *hua tea*, the 'favourite variety of sweet potato' was 'no longer found on Easter Island for it could not exist without the king who made it grow' (*ibid*). As one would expect, the paramount received certain first fruits and had some control over production: he could restrict or initiate harvesting, for instance. However, the general impressions of the more reliable observers suggested that the authority of the *ariki mau* was extremely limited, although there is very little information about the projects of different people, about successes and failures, which would enable us to see how claims of authority and relations of asymmetry and dependence were worked out in practice.

It is clear that beside the relationships between chiefs and people, another set of activities developed, which seem to have been a focus of society's attention, and which produced another sort of leader, the *tangata manu* or bird man. The cult revolved around a competition each year among some members of the Matatoa – the warrior clan 'in the ascendancy at any given time' (Routledge 1917: 339). Only those members of that clan who had been dreamt about by a shaman could compete. The competitors were usually prominent men of the clan; with various servants and many others they went up to the cult centre of Orongo, at the corner of the island near the rocky islets of Motunui and Motuiti, where each year the migratory sooty tern (*manu tara*) arrived to nest. Each competitor nominated a *hopu* or servant who actually participated in the race upon his behalf. The *hopu* went to the island and lived among the rocks, while the others lived in stone houses at Orongo, dancing every day. This race time was said to be one of 'intense excitement' (Thomson 1889: 483; cf. Routledge 1917: 340 n1). The first servant to secure an egg after the arrival of the birds tied it to his head in a basket and swam back to the island. According to Routledge 'the gods intervened in the hunt, so that the man who was not destined to win went right past the egg' (1917: 345). The new *tangata manu* shaved his head and painted it red, which was a *tapu* colour in many parts of Polynesia. The bird man was then secluded for five months, and was brought offerings of food which Routledge saw as 'the sole political advantages of victory' (1917: 348). The fact of seclusion certainly must have restricted the bird man's power to interfere in matters.

More significantly, the cult marks an overall shift towards warriors. Years were given the names of bird men: Routledge reported that 'the request to be given the names of as many bird years as possible met with an almost embarrassing response, eighty six being quoted straight away' and that there was a 'curious contrast' between this aspect of memory and 'the impossibility experienced in obtaining any satisfactory list of the "ariki" or chiefs' (1917: 352 & n). The construction of a time scale on the basis of eponymous archons or rulers' reigns says something about the stamp of a great person upon affairs – or at least about the construction of events at the time or retrospectively. In some sense bird men were more prominent than chiefs, even if not exactly central to society: the fact that numerous observers mistook the bird man competition for an election to the chiefship, or spoke of bird men as chiefs, testifies to the extent to which the chiefs proper were marginalized (e.g. Ollivier 1867: 255–6; Palmer 1870: 173). The fact that they were presented with the first sugar cane suggests a partial appropriation of the high chief's right to first fruits, although there was no basis in warrior activity for influence over nature.

With respect to practical influence, Roussel suggested that the king's 'authority was nil and entirely disregarded. It has passed entirely into the hands of the mata-toa who decided everything and carried on the war without beforehand consulting his majesty' (quoted in Métraux 1940: 135; cf. Thomson 1889: 472). There are many statements of this kind, virtually all of which are based on observation after 1862, when Peruvian slaving vessels kidnapped about 2,000 islanders to work on guano mines, including the then paramount chief (Maude 1982). Although a younger son survived to inherit the title, the catastrophe (compounded by epidemics) had a shattering and irreversible effect: even the bird man ceremonies were discontinued a few years later. It is thus very difficult to determine what kings and bird men did, and specifically how their forms of influence interacted in practice. The shape of leadership is perhaps less significant than the broader and deeper drift which the bird cult represented; there is no doubt that before the crisis this was a focus for popular excitement, entailing much organization and ceremony which the king had nothing to do with (Routledge, Ethnology, I: 101).

The ritual basis for chiefly encompassment thus seems to have co-existed with a dramatic erosion of the chieftainship. The archaeology of Rapanui makes this discrepancy understandable.

The island was probably first settled about AD 400 or 500. At that time

61

Rapanui was probably covered by an open dryland forest. There is relatively little information about prehistoric subsistence, but it is likely that, as in other parts of Polynesia, there was a diverse base incorporating animal husbandry, fishing, shell-fish collecting, and the cultivation of sugar cane, sweet potatoes, taro and bananas. The remarkable physical isolation and small size of Rapanui, however, meant that certain resources, such as wild seabirds, fish and shell-fish, were less abundant than elsewhere in Polynesia. There is a west to east continuum across the Pacific from floral and faunal abundance and diversity to impoverishment, and Easter Island was certainly at one extreme. The absence of a fringing coral reef meant in any case that marine resources were limited. Dogs and pigs were not introduced by Polynesian settlers or became rapidly extinct, no remains having been archaeologically recovered. The only introduced domestic animal was therefore the chicken which assumed an importance in subsistence and exchange it lacked elsewhere in Polynesia (McCoy 1979: 140; Flenley 1979; Kirch 1984: 264–78).

Despite these restricted resources a substantial population of perhaps 7,000 developed before AD 1000. There seem to have been relatively stable settlements of local descent groups which, from an early date, began to construct ceremonial centres, the most prominent elements of which were the famous statues. The especially impressive character of these figures has obscured the fact that they reflect a local development of east Polynesian *marae* (ritual centres), which were usually oriented towards a platform with some upright stones at one end. It is clear that the *moai* statues, like their less-striking counterparts in other structures, represented deified lineage ancestors, and that the ceremonies which took place on these sites related mainly to the distinction, celebration and commemoration of chiefly people and chieftainship. This was made apparent to members of Cook's second expedition, who visited Easter Island in March, 1774: 'they were erected to the memory of their chiefs; for they all had different Names and they always called them *Areekes*' (i.e. *ariki*) (Cook [1961]: 345; cf. Forster [1982], III: 469). Elsewhere in Polynesia the most important ceremonies which took place at *marae* were the installations of chiefs and paramounts, and rites for various stages in the lives of chiefly children (e.g. for Tahiti see Henry 1928: 157–96 *passim*). A chant concerning Tahitian *marae* concluded:

> It was the basis of royalty
> It awakened the gods
> It fixed the '*uru* girdle of sovereigns   (*ibid*: 151)[10]

On Rapanui much of the work of local descent groups in the earlier and middle periods of prehistory must have been dedicated to the construction of the temple precincts and statues. In their production, as well as in their subsequent ritual use, these most prominent structures directly reflected a society which revolved around, and was encompassed by, chieftainship.

This stable hierarchical order seems to have fallen apart as a consequence of overpopulation and landscape degradation. The burning of vegetation, perhaps associated with swidden cultivation, made erosion possible and, in the longer term forest regeneration impossible. Given the irregular but torrential pattern of rainfall in eastern Polynesia, this may have happened very quickly. The areas which would have supported cultivation were reduced, and the grassland formations which developed in place of earlier vegetation regimes were probably conducive to further erosion. Pollen studies have established that various trees which grew on the island in the past became extinct: there was certainly once a denser vegetation cover (McCoy 1979: 141). There was thus a serious contraction of the resource base, which was aggravated by the fact that the shortage of timber made it impossible to build large canoes, and thus restricted deep-sea fishing. Early visitors frequently noted the scarcity, smallness and 'very mean' character of the canoes (e.g. Roggeveen 1722 [1908]: 19; Cook [1961]: 352). The shortage of wood was evidently so acute that the islanders sometimes attempted to obtain it through barter with Europeans, which took place nowhere else in Polynesia (Dupetit-Thouars 1840–43, II: 227). A further difficulty arose from the absence of permanent streams, which precluded the intensification of agriculture through irrigation.

Given that Rapanui's resources were not, in any case, especially diverse or abundant, the deterioration of the environment must have produced widespread hunger and hardship. In particular cases this would have led to the rejection of individual chiefs but also evidently brought about the decline of chieftainship as such. Although the idiom of chiefly encompassment persisted in such forms as the chant quoted, and in the behavioural manifestations of *tapu*, these meanings must have been empty, given the failure of the chief to deliver the goods. The decline of the *ariki* was associated with the rise of the warriors, and an unstable and predatory system developed, in which warrior groups dispossessed others, and intense competition over declining resources developed. The change seems to have taken place about AD 1500 and is manifested archaeologically in thousands of obsidian spear points, and in the development of fortified dwellings in caves, noted by La Pérouse amongst others (1797, II: 86). Most statues were overthrown in this period; although the symbols of chiefly lines seem mainly to have been destroyed by enemy groups, the attack reflects broader rejection, since *marae* elsewhere in Polynesia were never desecrated in warfare (except in the context of the introduction of Christianity). This process seems still to have been going on in the late eighteenth and early nineteenth centuries, since some statues appear to have been knocked down between the visits of Cook (1774) and Kotzebue (1816) (Beechey 1831, I: 55). While many recent speculative writers have linked the statues with some foreign influence (such as an invasion of American Indians) most of the voyagers recognized that they had been built by the islanders, and La

Pérouse even noted that there must have been some change in the 'form of government' because there were no longer chiefs of such stature that so many men would occupy themselves in erecting a status to commemorate them (La Pérouse 1797, II: 86). This insight has, I think, been confirmed through archaeological work.

The bird man cult thus reflects not so much an opening-up, or loosening of a hierarchical order, which might ultimately have led to a new stratified system, but rather a distinct movement to a predatory warrior regime – which arose at the expense of the ancestral chiefly structure.[11]

Something like the social breakdown caused by hunger and overpopulation on Rapanui was witnessed by some early visitors to the Marquesas. Famine occured periodically: in the 1870s or 1880s, the missionary ethnographer Chaulet was told about six major events, which had names like 'suck bones' and 'withered fruit' (AMS: 22). The main cause of these crises was drought, which severely affected the staple, breadfruit, but the natural unreliability of precipitation was very much compounded by such social practices as the destruction (through ringbarking and similar means) of enemies' trees in war.

Between 1800 and 1803 hundreds of people died in some parts of Nukuhiva; whole valleys were said to be depopulated on 'Ua Pou. Many found the hazards of a canoe voyage more attractive than remaining on their island, and went to look for other islands dreamt about by their shamans 'a few days sailing distant' 'where plenty of food is abounding' (Robarts [1974]: 119). Although some people of property might have had food in reserve, reciprocity and distribution broke down. It was said that stronger preyed upon weaker, but since the absence of cannibalism motivated by hunger was asserted, and since no cases were ever documented, such talk was more likely an expression of the social disintegration produced by famine, rather than a description of events. Chaulet implies that two anti-social practices, cannibalism and incest – both signified by the word *kaikaia* – were conceptually compounded: 'they say that parents even eat their children' (AMS: 22).

Given these periodic crises, it might be expected that something similar to the rejection of chiefs on Rapanui would have transpired in the Marquesas. This is in fact so, although to a more limited extent. Chiefs were disconnected from the overall control of land, but did remain prominent and significant people, despite a dispersal of powers.

The distinctive feature of the Marquesan divergence from the hypothetical ancestral Polynesian pattern was that chiefs had lost control over the 'work of the gods'. There is no evidence that they were ever presented with first-fruits, nor that they ever performed any ceremonies connected with fertility. However, some *tau'a* (shamans) were thought to have 'power over the elements and seasons' and, more particularly, were 'firmly believed to dispense fertility to their Bread Fruit Trees' (Crook, Account: 137–8). It was they, therefore, who generally received gifts of food, and were recognized over whole islands, while chiefly authority was generally restricted to valley groups or often groups within valleys.[12]

Patterns in eastern Polynesian history

The Marquesan and Rapanui cases suggest a more general pattern of contrasts between such societies and those dominated by an encompassing chiefship or kingship. These can be represented as a pattern of transformation if it is supposed that the ancestral Polynesian system entailed an encompassing chiefly unity. Such an assumption could be justified on the basis of the very widespread distribution of first-fruits offerings, which directly manifest society's indebtedness to the chief who is virtually the giver of life and the cause of growth.

First, there is a general shift from the prominence of chiefs to the prominence of warriors. Secondly, the chief tends to become less of an orderly ruler and receiver of offerings, and more of a usurper or conqueror. This possibility is a variant on the first, and suggests that warrior activities are assimilated to the chiefship, whereas in the first case chiefs are more generally displaced by warriors. The Marquesas and Rapanui respectively reflect these divergent tendencies. The latter reflects a more extreme political rupture while the former seems less significant in itself. The third transformation is from a situation in which chiefs are ritual masters *par excellence*, and are the agents behind production and prosperity, to one in which shamans have moved out from the relatively restricted sphere of healing, have acquired the capacity to control the weather and crops, and have become much more significant in general. They also tend to displace 'official' priests (who are essentially the agents or servants of chiefs), and occupy the *marae*, the crucial sites of ritual activity. In the Marquesas (as well as on the island of Niue), chiefly displacement was more pronounced at this ritual level, and both shamanism in general, and a few individual shamans, became highly consequential.[13]

These shifts could be seen as 'devolutionary' in the sense that a centralized structure is diminished, but do not necessarily entail a diminution of inequality or stratification. It is quite implausible to represent these societies, as Goldman does, on a continuum between the more egalitarian 'traditional' and the 'stratified' systems. The central structure of chieftainship was clearly fractured in a radical way which would not permit more regionally-inclusive chiefdom-confederations or petty kingdoms to emerge. Societies such as the Marquesas represent a divergent step, which is more like to have been away from 'stratified' systems than towards them. If 'evolution' is seen as directional change, and 'devolution' its undoing, it is thus virtually impossible to understand these cases. The specific features of their histories,

65

of the changes which have been described, are obliterated by any model which imposes unilineal progressions.

Theoretical implications

The intermediate location of 'open' societies in Goldman's evolutionary sequence is plausible in his account because specific cases are misrepresented. In the Marquesas it is suggested that anyone could become a chief, and that chiefs did not have a great deal of authority anyway, but the disabling of chiefs in relation to vital rituals and property relations is not recognized. Thus the difference between a chief in this 'open' system and his counterpart in a 'stratified' society has the appearance of a quantitative difference: one has less power and the other rather more. It is easy to envisage that the former might somehow acquire more and end up resembling the latter. If attention is shifted away from this quantitative metaphor toward the special kinds of agency and capacities that certain privileged individuals have, it is obvious that difference is qualitative. The fact that the shamans take over a crucial capacity for vital ritual action cannot be incorporated into a model of evolution which is about increasing (or decreasing) stratification, but is central to one of the dominant patterns of political transformations in eastern Polynesia.

The difference between this overall interpretation and that of *Ancient Polynesian society* partly derives from theory, since in Goldman's work, as well as in evolutionary thought in general, evolution is closely identified with progressive movement towards increasing hierarchy and complexity. Although there is no explicit claim that this *must* be the case, the possibility of 'devolution' is neglected; moreover it seems that all change takes place along the continuum entailing increasing inequality, regional integration, and so forth; there is no space for divergent transformation which lacks a positive or negative evolutionary value.

The reappraisal of what eighteenth- and nineteenth-century Rapanui society represented was dependent on archaeological evidence. The use of this material – although truncated and illustrative in this case – amounts to something other than simply drawing on another body of relevant evidence, because it becomes possible to deal with longer-term change as a located historical process, rather than as an abstract difference between compared societies. The archaeological information is, of course, generally problematic and sketchy, and does not provide the basis of a fine-grained picture of the kind one might derive from historical or ethnographic materials. But there is a categorical distinction between a logic which uses a temporal metaphor to make a short cut through a tangle of differences between two societies which exist at the same time, and an argument which specifies the longer-term transformation of the one society. This society may be transformationally connected with others, but ancestry and divergence are specified in prehistory instead of abstractly imputed. The force of evolutionary argument should be its capacity to generate accounts of patterns of longer-term change. The construction of processes in prehistoric and historic sequences need not abandon this generalizing orientation, but can concretize and specify cases which are no longer subordinated to a logic of stages, ladders, or roads.

Differences between possible perspectives arise also from the form of evidence. Handy's propositions were derived from general impressions and accounts. An alternative description of Marquesan society can be based to a considerable extent on particular situations and events: an analysis, for example, of circumstances and disputes in the valley of Taiohae (on Nukuhiva) at the beginning of the nineteenth century generated a description of social relations around land which differed in crucial respects from the image derived from less particular accounts. Perhaps most interpretations seem to be based on a mixture of definite circumstances and generalities, but I will suggest later that 'events' in anthropological descriptions are not always as particular as they seem. In any case, the issue arises of the extent to which the distinct forms of apparently raw material give rise to a systematic divergence in interpretations.

There is a tendency for any general statement about society or culture (such as a 'rule' of behaviour) to be saturated by the particular colour of informants' or observers' constructions. Since generalized images of (collective) selves and others are important, such constructs must be attended to. But they do not necessarily reflect either more specific representations in social practice or social and political dynamics. On the other hand, images of events and particular circumstances speak more directly to an understanding of practices and patterns of change. The opposition here is not, of course, between ideology and actuality, or between internal, culture-bound models and scientific description. Deep-seated notions of various kinds animate all descriptions, whether they are enunciated by or elicited from tribal people, fabricated in the heat of a moment or with scientific detachment by intruders, and whether they allude to moments or propensities. I am not asserting that accounts of events and notions can be construed as transparent and opaque respectively, but the permeation and constitution of depiction is an uneven process which therefore permits different conclusions to be drawn from different kinds of descriptions, precludes others sometimes and perhaps some all the time. Some accounts can be read against the grain and turned perversely to an analyst's purpose, while others cannot, or smuggle peculiarities of their projection into the analysis. The circumstances in which cultural structures are manifested and played out in action can be drawn into a discussion of cultural and social dynamics, but the notions and metaphors of the structure itself often cannot. Ideas do not usually offer a commentary upon their own formation. Anthropologists must therefore attend to events

67

and practices, as well as representations. Some of the dominant images in the Easter Island and Marquesan cases did not differ substantially from those of other Polynesian societies. Only the examination of social relations, and of the salience of images in practice, could reveal the remarkable and distinctive characteristics of lives on those islands.

6

Travellers philosophical and unphilosophical

...several learned and ingenious works on the human species have appeared in the present age, written by philosophers, whose names alone should seem to be sufficient recommendation. I have, however, early observed, that, being misled by the vague reports of unphilosophical travellers, which they have sometimes wilfully changed and moulded, to suit their own opinions; their systems, though ever so ingenious, are seldom agreeable to nature. It appears indeed to be the general fault of these writers, to study mankind only in their cabinets; or, at best, to observe no other than highly civilized nations...

Johann Reinhold Forster, *Observations made on a voyage round the world* (1778)

These criticisms are reminiscent of the repudiation in early twentieth-century ethnography of speculative 'armchair' anthropology. The anthropology which was confined to book cabinets was not, of course, opposed by a whole professional school of more grounded studies, but a great deal of writing of various sorts was drawn more directly from experience among 'savages'. Much of my criticism thus far has in fact played upon a matching of twentieth-century ethnographies of 'traditional' societies against a knowledge which draws on allusions and descriptions in a curious array of earlier publications and documents. One of the arguments of this essay is that it is vital to know things that can only be known through such fragments and constructions, and that it is vital to link such sources with later, apparently more rounded professional ethnographies. This assertion might seem to be unproblematic, but runs against a deeply-held anthropological view that older authorities, and especially missionary accounts, are of limited and dubious value, being at best unsystematic and at worst deeply prejudiced.[1]

Antipathies between anthropologists and missionaries in the field have various grounds, such as an apparent conflict of interest: missionaries are thought to be eradicating the traditions and pagan rituals which anthropologists want to study. Mission practice has been, by definition, interventionist, and has often invited criticism for various reasons. But the methodological exclusion of certain kinds of information has a different basis in the larger configuration of anthropological discourse. A central feature of the discipline's practice has been and is fieldwork carried out by a trained investigator. Whether this is regarded as a rigorous process, or, as in Geertz's more honest account, as a tentative matter of 'finding one's feet' (chapter 2), the form of learning is represented as the only significant source of anthropological knowledge. The implication in Geertz's account was that neither those who experienced a situation without an ethnographer's inquisitive orientation, nor those who reflected upon social circumstances without such experience, could arrive at any distinctively anthropological understanding. The perception is thus that analysis and interpretation are directly derived from a method, or rather, a celebrated activity which is constitutive of 'the anthropologist' as a person and a practitioner. The difficulty, though, is that some kinds of crucial information about particular cultures cannot be obtained through fieldwork; nor can they be obtained by dipping into a few historical sources in a way which is entirely marginal to a fieldwork project. An adequate historical account frequently depends upon much rigorous and extensive research, yet serious historical research is devalued in two ways: as a practice, it is not embedded in the interpretive effort to translate culture, and lacks the experiential character of fieldwork (which may be privileged from a variety of positivist, materialist and interpretive perspectives); secondly, it draws upon accounts which are taken to be flawed, partial, ideologically-tainted and generally inadequate to the construction of professional ethnography. Since the 'methodological' issue of the status of various kinds of early sources is directly connected with the 'theoretical' issue of whether a historical anthropology is desirable or practical, the basis of this generalized exclusion must be examined.

The characteristics of missionary ethnography

Malinowski dismissed the missionary contribution, which he claimed was exemplified by such gross misstatement as the following: 'We teach lawless men to become obedient, inhuman men to love, and savage men to change' (C. W. Abel, in Malinowski 1922: 10n). His criticism was specifically that the notion that the savage was governed merely by instincts or 'unchecked passions' failed to recognize the 'strict code of behaviour and good manners' which in fact prevailed. While it could not be disputed that certain missionaries were entirely obtuse, it is most unlikely that any actually thought that there was no regulation of conduct in primitive societies. Such extravagant claims, where made, are frequently found to be undermined by material in the same missionary text. But Malinowski quotes from evangelical propaganda as though it represented and expressed missionary under-standing. He does not even mention that the book he quotes, *Savage life in New Guinea*, was aimed at children. (The first sentences of the main text are: 'British boys and girls! I want to introduce you to my friend, the strange wild inhabitant of New Guinea' [Abel 1902: 11].) It would be remarkable if works of this kind, which were produced mainly to stimulate fund-raising, exhibited anything like scholarly detachment. The fact that the sentence Malinowski quoted was in the 'before and after' form, expressing the transformation from savage to Christian, exposes the central polemical intent. The striking contrasts which were meant to be apparent to readers of the missionary literature from the fields in which the Gospel had already taken hold were a promise that funds expended in extending the endeavour would certainly bring forth results (the agricultural metaphor was frequently employed in this context). To treat this literature, often edited and worked up by metropolitan writers, as a serious reflection of the knowledge of missionaries in the field, is like equating the claims of election manifestos with the analyses of party researchers. However, even in such works much of the description is far closer to conventional anthropological writing than writers such as Malinowski would permit one to expect. One section introduces in a straightforward if elementary way the differences between 'Papuan' and more familiar families:

A partition about three feet high divides the house in two; the front portion being reserved for the male members of the family, and the back – which is smaller – being at the disposal of the women. A house is never occupied only by a man and his wife and family. Aunts, uncles, and cousins of many removes are included in the family circle. Relationships are not so simple as they are with us. On the wife's side especially the ties are very close. For instance, if you were a New Guinea boy, or girl, your mother's brother would rank as your father, and her sister as your mother; your first cousins on your mother's side would actually be your brothers and sisters, and so on. So that if you enquire of a New Guinea householder how his family is made up, you find it includes relations having strong claims upon him, though they are only distantly connected from our benighted way of thinking. (Abel 1902: 28–9)

Malinowski failed to acknowledge that a certain ethnographic curiosity lay behind the writings of missionaries. This was loosely linked with mission objectives, and it is occasionally explicitly stated that native systems should be understood in order that they might be changed or subverted, but this was as much a way of legitimizing the interest as a real indication of connections which were in fact generally tenuous. It is sometimes clear that the writers saw themselves having a thirst for knowledge which was detached from any instrumental purpose. In the Preface to the second edition of his synthesis, *Polynesian researches*, William Ellis noted that various early reports had 'excited a strong desire to obtain additional information' relating to various subjects such as 'the nature of [the Polynesians'] ancient institutions' (1831, I: xix). Since great changes were taking place, principally consequent on the adoption of Christianity, knowledge of former ways and circumstances was thought to be fading.

The present, therefore, seems to be the only time in which a variety of facts, connected with the former state of the Inhabitants, can be secured; and to furnish, as far as possible, an authentic record of these, and thus preserve them from oblivion, is one design which the Author has always kept in view. (*ibid*: xix–xx; cf. Gill 1894: 8–9)

Ellis noted further that the relative simplicity of Polynesian society afforded particular 'facilities' for observing the 'essential characteristics' and 'tendencies' of idolatry 'which could not be obtained in a more advanced state of society' (*ibid*). This particular description was thus intended to serve a more general knowledge of heathen societies.[2] To some extent, a model for investigation, the use of informants, and data collection developed through language work, because, in many cases, competence in previously unrecorded languages was absolutely essential for effective mission work.[3] In some instances, missionaries' diaries make it clear that obtaining lists of words led them to other topics such as names of deities, and to other activities such as compiling censuses (e.g. Darling 1834–35).

Accurate reportage was regarded as a virtue and it is clear that some missionary descriptions of particular beliefs or customs were the products of specific inquiries rather than observation which was incidental to missionary activity. This gave rise to numerous works of relatively extensive and precise description, some of which contained very little in the way of mission propaganda. The criteria which legitimate such writings as pieces of adequate description are sometimes foregrounded: a 'correct and reliable' account of 'manners and customs, occupations and surroundings [and] modes of thought' among other things, will consist of knowledge gathered in a particular way, as James Gilmour notes in his Preface to *Among the Mongols*:

[The book] is not a missionary's report nor a traveller's diary, nor a student's compilation, but has for its source things seen, heard and experienced by me while travelling with natives in the desert, sharing with them the hospitality of the wayside tent, taking my turn in the night-watch against thieves, resting in the comparative comfort of the portable cloth travelling tent, or dwelling as a lodger in their more permanent abodes of trellis-work and felt while engaged first of all in learning the language and acquainting myself with the country, and afterwards in the prosecution of my missionary duties. (1883: 5–6)

Gilmour proceeds to indicate from which area his knowledge derives, and reiterates that the combination of linguistic competence and careful observation is the basis of a secure description. This is, of course, highly reminiscent of Malinowski's later insistence upon the importance of the ethnographer's intimate contact with the native people (with the implications of friendship and shared hardship), but reflects a far more general device of authentication and justification in descriptive works about foreign parts or peoples: it is crucial that the author's singular qualifications be initially specified, since these provide the basis for belief in the account. These are sometimes even expressed in titles such as *Seventeen years among the Dayaks* or *Travels in Africa*, which sometimes distinguished a work of personal observation from one of secondary compilation. The distinctive feature of this mechanism in Gilmour's and Malinowski's books is that the special character of the knowledge is defined by a series of exclusions: the work is not merely based on personal observation, but draws rather on a depth of familiarity beyond that which casual travellers could conceivably acquire. This is signalled in Malinowski by the break with the company of other white men and in Gilmour by the variety of everyday Mongol experience he has shared. The tendency in contemporary anthropology has been to lengthen the introductory sections which convey the personal side of fieldwork; this amounts to an unrestrained elaboration of the more general literary construct and makes an uncompromising assertion of validity in the guise of a more innocent sketch of the circumstances of work.[4]

There is a more specific supposition that missionary descriptions are worthless in so far as they deal with religious matters because of the specific antipathy of the writers to non-Christian religious beliefs. In fact, there are some cases where the experience of missionary observers obviously led them to believe that pagan magic was efficacious in practice (e.g. Marzan 1908). Europeans other than missionaries were frequently convinced that sorcery worked: Edward Robarts concluded a description with the words 'this I have seen and know to be true' ([1974]: 255). He had reason to feel threatened, because a hostile Frenchman also resident on Nukuhiva had attempted to acquire knowledge of the rites in order to kill him. Published missionary accounts usually make passing references to the false or objectionable character of specific beliefs, or the 'contradictory absurdities' of the whole system (Williams 1884: 211), but such statements cannot be regarded as premises or structuring principles for the overall exposition. If this was the case, the discourse would emphasize discontinuities and lack of coherence, but the systematizing drive of western knowledge generally defeated this impulse, with the result that descriptions of 'pagan' religious beliefs did attempt to ground specific observances or rites in frameworks such as ancestor worship which made them sensible in their context.[5]

The distinction in the corpus of missionary work between unpublished letters and diaries and what was passed on to the public must here be appreciated. Much soul-searching and prejudice about indigenous systems does appear in private papers, but a great deal of ethnographic and linguistic discussion for its own sake is also found. In published form this tended to be directed didactically, although early periodicals often presented missionaries' letters or journal extracts from the field in an abbreviated but relatively unmodified form. But there is a sharper gap between such texts and later mass-distribution publications like that quoted by Malinowski, which are clearly composed and organized with a central didactic aim. Some notion of rigour lay behind the preparation of such essays as the 1800 'Account of the Marquesas Islands'[6] which seem to have been conceived as purely scientific; it was explicitly noted that some things (such as homosexual practices) might be mentioned in such a 'private' discourse which presumably would not have gone further.

The form of ethnographic knowledge

Many specific questions about the merits and uses of particular accounts must arise in the practice of research. The perspicacity of writers varied, and the nature of their work sometimes demanded greater or less attention to such things as linguistics and ethnography. These issues obviously cannot be pursued at a general level. Judgements must be made in particular cases, and depend as much upon a researcher's objectives – what he or she hopes to extract from a source – as upon the particular features of that text. My emphasis is rather that this species of 'pre-anthropological' work has not deserved its discredited status; that work has been rejected because of a gross category to which it was assigned, rather than on the basis of criteria which would also have applied to modern anthropological descriptions. As I stressed in chapter 2, this was, of course, integral to the professionalization of anthropology and the exclusion of unqualified persons whose experience and linguistic competence might otherwise rival what Malinowski called 'the Ethnographer's magic' (1922: 6). Moreover, the charge of so-called bias fails to specify particular properties of these sorts of knowledge, which are at once accounts in their own right and 'source materials' in various contexts.

Although the distinction between synchrony and diachrony might be seen as a product of modern linguistic thought, late eighteenth- and nineteenth-century accounts of Pacific societies were frequently divided into a narrative of a stream of events and what amounted to a synchronic exposition – not exactly of culture or grammar, but of manners, customs, and general attributes. In the most important early account of Tonga, that based on William Mariner's participant observation between 1806 and 1810, about two-thirds is devoted to Mariner's shipwreck, difficulties, involvement in war, adoption, and experiences in general, while most of the rest concerns 'manners, customs and sentiments' described under the following headings: Rank in society, religious, civil and professional; Religion; Religious Ceremonies; Knowledge; Dress; Domestic habits; Pastimes; Music and poetry; and Language (Martin 1827, II: 81). Similarly, the Russians' accounts of the Marquesas were divided into descriptions of meetings with chiefs, barter, excursions inland, and so forth, and generalized accounts of habitations – war – cannibalism – productions – religion – tabus – etc. (Krusenstern 1813; Lisiansky 1814).[7]

Discussion in these expository sections has an 'ethnographic' rather than a narrative character because the objects are categories or totalities about which general statements are made. In Crook's 'Account of the Marquesas Islands' (1800), types of priest, forms of rank and 'usages' are detached from any particular occurrences or manifestations. In a much later manuscript description, Chaulet's 'Notices géographiques, enthnographiques...', we find a similar work of induction, distinction and elaboration. In a chapter on religion, priests and priestesses are discussed under the major categories of *tuhuka* (who chanted and offered sacrifices) and *tau'a* (shamans; defined as those especially charged with making known the god's will and seeing it effected). Eleven different types of *tau'a* are identified, and many rituals such as particular sacrifices are described:

To obtain a good catch, the fishermen begin by taking a long basket woven from green coconut leaves to some sacred place, where they hang it up with a long *ute* strap, so the gods of fishing felt to live there will be favourable. This is called *hami oa*. Then they prepare pastes of *poke* and *kaku* [breadfruit-based preparations] which they take with them to the place where they want to fish...[etc.].   (Chaulet, Notices: 145)

This is a discourse of procedures and rules, not one of singularities, observed moments, of things which happened once only. The question of happening is in fact suppressed in a domain of generalized possibilities and situations: fishermen do this when they go fishing; the sorcerer does this when he wants to kill; they conduct this ceremony when a chiefly girl menstruates for the first time. The reader's apprehension bypasses particular sorcerers and occasions, and seizes onto the general domain of procedures, like a rule book. The tense and register distinguishes ethnographic writing from descriptions which do not venture into the space of partial abstraction, which lack the vision of a whole array of seeming possibilities.

This mode of writing is found in the accounts of voyagers as well as those of missionaries. In some cases European deserters resident on islands interpreted and supplied intricate local information which could not possibly have been obtained or understood in the course of brief ships' visits. But frequently – and especially in the earliest period – there was no-one to act in such a capacity, and explorers' interpretations are discernibly insecure. In the voyage literature we therefore find the form of ethnographic knowledge in the absence of its basis – linguistic competence and protracted and intimate intercourse with a people. These requirements are axiomatic in modern anthropology, but were virtually recognized much earlier. Cook, for example, was aware of the limitations of the material gathered on his own voyages. According to James Boswell, who dined with Cook and other members of the Royal Society in April, 1776, 'he candidly confessed...that he and his companions who visited the south sea islands could not be certain of any of the information they got...their knowledge of the language was so imperfect they required the aid of their senses, and any thing which they learnt about religion, government or traditions might be quite erroneous' (quoted in Cook [1961]: 234 n5). Boswell himself apparently 'fancied going to one of the islands for three years to learn the language and bring home a full account' but expected that if he did so he should receive a 'handsome pension for life' from the government (*ibid*).

Of course, the kind of fieldwork envisaged here was not conducted until the early twentieth century. But what distinguished modern ethnography was its professional orientation, rather than any essential difference in the basis of its knowledge:[8] as is well known, many missionaries possessed local knowledge and linguistic competence based on decades of experience, rather than one or two years. In the Pacific, certain writers other than missionaries could draw on experiences which closely approximated the ideal of 'immersion' in the local society, since these European deserters or beachcombers acted as warriors for chieftains, married into their families, became tattooed, and, most importantly, through their own action and manipulation, developed a practical understanding and mastery of (altered) indigenous tactics and strategies. These individuals were generally less educated than the missionaries and hardly any wrote ethnographic accounts in the stricter sense, although there are many books with titles such as *Shipwreck and adventures among the South Sea Islanders … giving an account of their feasts, massacres, etc.* But in certain cases books were written with the assistance of an educated man, or by him on the basis of interviews and discussion. The most famous example is certainly the *Account of the natives of the Tonga Islands*, which was written by John Martin, a doctor, on the basis of information from William Mariner, who had lived in Tonga from 1806 to 1810. Mariner was only 15 when he survived the capture of his ship by the Tongans and, in the view of H. E. Maude, 'assimilated the Tongan culture as naturally as he would have his own at the same impressionable age' (1968: 173). In these cases, the discursive construction of ethnography is found in conjunction with what might be seen as its proper experiential basis.

The combination of these elements does not, of course, ensure that a description is either valid or insightful. The point is rather that the specific problems of pre-anthropological accounts of native peoples thus cannot be condensed into the absence of the elements of proper ethnography. The questions which arise are as diverse as those which arise from the different sorts of professional ethnography. No methodological distinction can be made between a missionary ethnography and some product of modern research which a synthesis or comparative study, draws upon. A correlate of this equation is, however, that early ethnographic accounts cannot simply be seen as 'sources' or raw material. Since my suggestion about Goldman's work was partly that complications arose from inattention towards the properties of museum ethnography, problems of the same order might arise in the incorporation of earlier materials. These issues arise in certain ways in properly 'ethnographic' discourses and in certain other ways in relation to apparently less refined narratives of 'feasts, massacres, etc.'

In late eighteenth- and early nineteenth-century ethnography, physical and social attributes were not usually radically distinguished in descriptions of either individuals or peoples. In fact, the array of behavioural traits had a coherent base in a sort of notion of ethnicity which consisted in physical and mental character. This was sometimes achieved through individualizing the 'race':[9] the 'Feejeean' or the 'Nukuhivan' is the type possessing attributes. 'The native of Senegal is characterized by a timorous disposition...' (Forster 1778: 227). This way of speaking makes it possible to characterize collectivities in terms of attitudes and proclivities (this also appears in modern writing, as in Geertz's opposition between the Javanese and Morrocan characters cum cultural types [1968]). It is thus possible to suggest that dispositions are engendered without reference to a collective mind or culture. Even where statements are pluralized, observation is still essentially in terms of propensities. A review of the first edition of Mariner's *Tonga* brings out the kind of construction which specific information fed:

We behold in them the natives of a country placed under a vertical sun, endowed with natural advantages both mental and corporeal, and with a degree of hardihood to endure and valour to undertake, that are equal to whatsoever is known of the inhabitants of the most vigour-giving climates; and who, in their capabilities of attainment, are to be ranked with the highest classes of our species. At the same time, we see them in a statement of society and of morals so barbarous that they must be regarded as savages. Their great virtue is that which the Romans esteemed pre-eminent, *Fortitude*; while their great vice is the one most common to barbarians, and of all evil qualities the most base, *Treachery*. Yet, such as they are, the description given of them frequently reminds us of the heroes in the Iliad.   (Anon. 1817: 359)

The earlier nineteenth-century metropolitan interest was thus one which constituted national types and noticed parallels between other places and various moments in classical history and mythology. Such observations might take the forms of naive comparisons while others articulated the implicit evolutionary logic. These notions influenced depictions of other parts of the world in art and theatre[10] and also, no doubt, had some influence on those who went out to the Pacific and subsequently themselves wrote about Melanesian and Polynesian peoples. But was it therefore the case that a rather silly set of interests amounted to an ideology which profoundly distorted nineteenth-century representations of Pacific islanders? No, because the discourse was neither unitary nor homogenous: there was no specific construction which permeated it as a whole, and the various texts were full of incompatible constructions. One reviewer of a later memoir of experiences on a central Polynesian atoll complained that 'we have generally but vague notions [of Pacific Islanders] compounded of the incongruous images of cannibalism and Captain Cook' (Anon. 1868: 55). So far from imposing stereotypes, speculative anthropology in fact provided a foil for the descriptive authority of those who had actually visited the Pacific:

...obedience is understood as well as tyranny, and the despotism and wantonness of the chiefs is equalled only by the correspondent timidity and submission of the people. Philosophers are much mistaken who build systems of natural liberty. Rousseau's savage, a being who roves the woods according to his own will, exists no where but in his writings.   (Turnbull 1813: 201)

A more specific problem which underlay the discussion of native propensities has already been mentioned: many writers failed to recognize that the characteristics which were projected as the attributes of the native type arose specifically in the circumstances of confrontation or contact. Thus the extensive sexual contacts between Polynesian women and sailors – which appear to have been initially motivated by a desire to bear children fathered by apparently divine and powerful beings (Sahlins 1981: 40; Ralston 1988) – generated an image of 'libertines' in the writings of Bougainville and many others.[11] In Portman's account of Andamanese culture the logic emerges in a curious and qualified form:

> They are gentle and pleasant to each other ... they are certainly cruel, and are jealous, treacherous and vindictive ... [but] they are affectionate to their wives, and their worst qualities are kept for strangers. I have often likened them to English country schoolboys of the labouring classes ... (1899, I: 33)

Here the context of a kind of behaviour is recognized, but it is still supposed that a particular element, such as 'treachery', is internal to the native, and prior to any particular incident. Portman recognized that these attributes were only to be discerned in the interaction between Andamanese and foreign intruders, but nevertheless saw this simply as the circumstance under which the traits emerge or surface, rather than their cause or origin.

Cook himself attempted to contextualize what he saw as the misrepresentation of Tahitian female character:

> great Injustice has been done the Women of Otaheite and the Society Isles, by those who have represented them without exception as ready to grant the last favour to any man who will come up to their price. But this is by no means the case; the favours of Maried women and also the unmarried of the better sort, are as difficult to obtain here as in any other Country whatever. Neither can the charge be understood indiscrimenately of the unmaried of the lower class. That there are Prostitutes here as well as in other Countrys is very true, perhaps more in proportion and such were those who came on board the Ship to our people and frequented the Post we had on shore ... On the whole a stranger who visits England might with equal justice draw the Characters of the women there, from those which he might meet with on board the Ships in one of the Naval Ports, or in the Purlieus of Covent Garden & Dury [*sic*] lane. (Cook [1961]: 238–9)

The fact that it is possible to criticize the projection of characteristic attributes indicates that, although this kind of proposition has a systematic presence in early accounts, and although the logic is erroneous from the viewpoint of modern anthropology, the flaw does not obliterate the value of the description. The analysis of the context and the critique of the judgement in fact make it possible to read a 'source' in part as a commentary on its own process of observation and extrapolation. It is also possible to turn its observations, once reconstituted, towards other ends. This work of reading is no different to what one does in drawing structuralist interpretations from

78

(another writer's) functionalist ethnography, or materialist insights from accounts of myth-making.

The general claim here is that the work of predecessors – whether distant or recent – cannot be written off on the grounds of theoretical or ideological contamination. Functionalist premises do not animate or permeate the entire fabric of a functionalist ethnography. The ethnographic depiction is not generally or uniformly invalid because a major or the principal interpretative threads are rejected. Descriptions can, in any case, be reread into something else, and turned away from imputed errors. My critique of the ahistorical aspect of anthropological writing suggests that problems generated by that absence go deeper than has been previously acknowledged, but does not thereby deny the value of the whole range of ahistorical scholarship. The point is rather that specific misinterpretations are consistently generated. This sort of criticism and evaluation is equally appropriate for 'pre-anthropological' and 'professional' predecessors.

This line of argument is necessary because there is an idea of a progressive movement in anthropological method characterized by certain sharp breaks (notably Malinowski), as well as more gradual shifts, toward fuller knowledge, based particularly upon 'the greater length and intensity of field studies and the greater attention paid by ethnographers to language learning' (A. Hooper 1985: 4). This is associated with a notion that earlier ethnographies or pre-anthropological works are simply displaced by more recent studies which are more securely based (meaning that they conform more particularly to criteria of merit which happened to be current, which at various times have privileged the collection of genealogies, of quantitative data, of particular types of linguistic material, etc.). It would make little sense for anyone within anthropology to deny that there has been progress in methods at some level. My claim is rather that earlier forms of ethnography have been discredited to an extent which is quite out of proportion to the actual differences between such texts and modern anthropological writing. The exercise of comparative evaluation, of asserting the merits of older or more recent researches, is, however, ultimately misguided because it treats the ethnographies of different epochs as substitutable for one another. Thus a sensitive recent symbolic study might replace cruder museum ethnography; a historically-oriented anthropologist might invert the judgements and privilege a missionary source over something done later. A 'restudy' can be made of an ethnographic locality twenty or thirty years later. There is an element of likeness presupposed in this substitution, which should be seen as misconceived because the ethnographies are not in fact accounts of the same thing. Earlier sources may certainly have a more plausible claim to reflect a traditional or pre-contact situation, but somewhere like Central Fiji in 1876 cannot be identified with the same place in the 1920s or 1980s – unless there is a notion of 'Fijian culture' which stands outside time and history.[12]

Beyond ethnography: 'incidents' and incidental references

All general statements suppose some suppression of difference from time to time or place, between cases and various people's versions. Even an account of some particular sequence of events is likely to reflect some agglomeration of accounts which obliterates the differences between distinct perspectives. Propositions about the sorts of behaviour which should or do take place between certain classes of relatives presumably depend on numerous observations and statements. Questions can be raised at any point in an analysis about whether particular moments in the suppression of difference are desirable. The answer will depend primarily on the interests and purposes implicit in a piece of writing. In some cases discussing the differences between two towns or villages might contribute nothing more than mindless empirical elaboration; in other cases such detail and contrasts might fuel an analysis of economic and political processes in a region (cf. C. White 1981). The divergent claims of different informants might equally be inconsequential or crucial (cf. Young 1983: 3, 53, *passim*). Suppressing the difference between 'Fijian culture' as apprehended at certain dates is thus a variant upon a more general and necessary movement, and might be seen to be no more problematic or pernicious than other constructions which smudge their sources. But the content of these inductive steps varies. In some cases, the exclusion of variation simply precludes a certain kind of analysis: how children and adults see the house, or work, differently. Other dimensions of difference are more fundamental, and play a part in the constitution of notions which are *already internal* to an analysis. Anthropological explanations which attempt to go beyond an account of the positional order of social or cultural features at a particular time must raise questions about the logic of transformations, of how a system in a particular place arises when other possibilities apparently exist. A study of palm economies in eastern Indonesia, for instance, revealed that a pattern of difference which might have been explained in terms of ecological adaptations can be accounted for far more persuasively through reference to the history of local political conflicts, Dutch trading activities, and various other factors (Fox 1977). The suppression of the historical process thus leads to error rather than simply omission. This is what can be seen to take place in Handy's misinterpretation of Marquesan chieftainship.

If it is acknowledged that differences over time matter, then early accounts become significant in a way which has nothing to do with the extent to which they conform or fail to conform with notions of what ethnography should be.

Societies beyond Europe and the 'civilized' centres were potential objects of research for professional anthropologists because prior contacts and expressions of force had established ways into them, and perhaps pacified warriors or extended colonial jurisdiction. In general, the people to be known were controlled to some degree. Intrusive institutions such as missions and administrative posts were easily recognized as isolable entities by anthropologists and might be mentioned but were cut out of the central ethnographic discussion. There was a sense that the consequences of intrusion could be traced around such discrete manifestations of penetration. The subtraction of these specific effects from the overall picture left an image of the traditional. In all cases of interaction between traders or settlers and indigenous populations, there are, however, more subtle processes whereby external effects generate internal change. A variety of early accounts are significant because they speak directly about the events which constitute such change, about the conditions which make description possible and always already transform the thing described. The facts spoken of do not fall within the domain of ethnological subject-matter: they are events which happen sometimes once, sometimes again and again, not 'customs', institutions or symbols. The cultural dimensions of such acts or accidents may sometimes be suggested by renderings in oral or written sources, but may not be overtly acknowledged.

If notions or practices constitute a tradition which is cognized as such, both indigenous peoples and observers may have an interest in disguising the causal relations between the form of culture and historical processes, as Keesing acknowledged in a Solomon Islands case:

I arrived among the Kwaio announcing my intention to record their customs. I gradually learned that the Kwaio had sacrificed and prayed to enlist me in their cause, as an American who was going to 'write' and 'straighten out' Kwaio custom (*kastom*) for them ... As long as I collected genealogies, recorded stories of ancestors, explored the structures of kinship, feasting, and exchange, recorded ancestrally policed taboos, and sat in on weekly meetings where 'chiefs' ... debated intricacies of land rights and customary law and adjudicated in litigation, my work and the expectation of traditionalist (male) leaders meshed closely ... Indeed, their politically motivated commitment to (the impossible task of) codifying customary law and my theoretically motivated commitment to (the impossible task of) writing a 'cultural grammar' in the manner of Goodenough, Conklin, and Frake doubtless, in retrospect, entailed a good deal of mutual cooptation.   (1985: 28–9)

This also suggests that the processes behind whatever configurations have been rendered 'traditional' cannot necessarily be discerned internally. This must be the case to an especially marked extent if exchanges and interactions with outsiders have a long history.

The earliest contacts between representatives of a European world and islanders entailed various sorts of barter, theft, and exchange – acts which effected movements of objects between ships and island societies. Much has been written on the technological 'stone to steel' transition, but rather less on local constructions of apparently utilitarian objects of desire, which were often assimilated into indigenous categories of prestigious or ritually significant things. While this literature has perhaps therefore sustained a restricted view of the ramifications of change, more complex questions about political relationships and hierarchy certainly emerge if the importation of things which might loosely be described as 'valuables' is considered. The circulation of indigenous prestige objects was frequently restricted in certain ways. Their uses were linked with hierarchy and particular elite strategies, which could hardly have been sustained had supplies and distribution not been controlled, or if overall quantities precluded monopolization. In so far as hierarchical relations themselves were constituted and perpetuated through the use of particular gift-objects, one would expect the structure to be transformed by any significant mutation in patterns of exchange – such as the sudden availability of a new supply of the objects.

Throughout Fiji, the 'greatest of valuables' was the whale's tooth or *tabua*. Gifts of *tabua* were and are essential elements of many ceremonies connected with marriage, death, birth and chiefly installation. Teeth could be used to solicit services, and initiate political alliances or cycles of exchange. These ceremonial uses are extensively described in numerous twentieth-century ethnographies (e.g. Thompson 1940; Sahlins 1962; Nayacakalou 1975). None of these authors mention the fact that, whereas *tabua* are now widely distributed, and are used in commoner villages as well as in chiefly centres, this cannot have been the case in the past, because the only sources for teeth were whales which were occasionally stranded on coral reefs. As this seems to have happened more often in Tonga than Fiji, supplies depended on external contacts rather than what might be collected locally. Attempts to form even rough ideas of the numbers of *tabua* in circulation at earlier times would be futile, but there is no doubt that these objects were extremely scarce before contact with Europeans. Very soon afterwards, the situation was very different, as Clunie has explained:

With the onset of the sandal wood trade from 1804, some thousands of Sperm Whale teeth and of elephant and walrus tusks cut to resemble Whale teeth were imported by Yankee, Colonial (New South Wales) and East India traders, who instantly recognized their incredibly high intrinsic worth in Viti [early Fiji].
(1986: 176–7; cf. Hooper 1982: 85–9)

The quantity introduced was certainly very considerable: an 1809 newspaper item indicates that one ship alone was carrying 190 teeth for trade in Fiji (Im Thurn and Wharton 1925: 200). The significance of the number emerges if it is noted that one of the largest tributary prestations recorded only ten, and that one tooth was sufficient as a bounty for an assassination (Williams 1931 [1843], I: 145; Brewster 1922: 27–8; cf. Hooper 1982: 93).

It is moreover clear that there have been a whole series of changes in both the volume of external supplies and the manner of their importation. After the dramatic initial increase associated with the trade in sandalwood (stands of which were rapidly exhausted), there was an interval when foreign traders were uninterested in extracting any resources from Fiji; contact was renewed when a trade in *bêche-de-mer*, also destined for the Chinese market, developed and brought in new supplies of whale teeth. Clunie argued that the great increase in numbers of *tabua* permitted chiefs, who apparently successfully monopolized the objects, to intensify and elaborate their political activity: expansive efforts and conflict between chiefly confederations therefore increased dramatically in the first decades of the nineteenth century. In the longer term, however, Steven Hooper suggests that the use of whale teeth has been 'democratized' (1982: 87), but it is not clear precisely whether a range of ceremonial acts, or specifically the use of *tabua* in those acts, have ceased to be exclusively the prerogatives of chiefs. In the earlier period it is clear that the supply of whale teeth was itself the cause of change, whereas subsequent patterns of distribution may have arisen as much because of transformations in the hierarchical system as because of qualitative shifts in the supply of valuables.

These changes do not all belong to the distant past. Earlier in the twentieth century many *tabua* were taken out of Fiji by Europeans passing through or returning home, but the decline in numbers was arrested when their export was prohibited; there was in fact an increase, because some hundreds were imported from Scotland and distributed by the administration in the 1950s (Hooper 1982: 86). In a study of economic development, Belshaw implied that there was a more general government policy of 'injecting cheap supplies from time to time' which, he argued, permitted 'ceremonial inflation' (1964: 150); this was disapproved of because it hindered 'the growth of the economy'.

It would be manifestly misleading to suggest in this kind of case that a system might be identified and analysed primarily in non-historical, internal terms. This would situate the causes of elements of the system internally, when such elements are in fact clearly the products of the conjunction of external causes and internal dynamics. Even prior to European contact, it is clear that changing relations with other island groups (such as Tonga) had an impact on Fijian political structures.

Such incidents as constituted the barter which brought whale teeth into Fiji cannot thereby be seen as merely 'incidental'. They bear directly on problems at the core of anthropological inquiry. The implication of this for the ascription of various statuses to kinds of sources of information is that accounts which have a strictly ethnographic character – such as a modern study or something like Chaulet's description of Marquesan beliefs – cannot be seen to constitute a core of material to which references to events are secondary. This logic is inevitable if the anthropological object is defined in a way which excludes change or renders it subsequent to native culture, the primary entity. The tendency in anthropological writing has been to dismiss accounts of moments or events because they apparently fail to bear upon strictly ethnographic questions, or because, in so far as they do, they are wrong. Firth cites a sailor's mistaken belief that Tikopia men were castrated as proof of 'the utter worthlessness of casual observation derived from the stay of a day or so which the *Southern Cross* and other vessels make' (1936: 408). This criticism is, of course, a motivated one, in that it separates anthropological knowledge from the error-prone vision of stray travellers. It is also legitimate, since it would be remarkable if ethnographers (and other resident foreigners) did not have a better knowledge of local matters than visitors who had only had sporadic contact with a population. But this is not the point. Most of the people who visit places, whether inhabited by tribal people or others, on continents or islands, do so because they want to do something, which frequently entails transactions or other social acts which have effects. What they say about what they do may be crucial, no matter how obtuse or misguided their overall understanding may be.

A trader visiting an atoll near the Society Islands might note that pigs were received 'in exchange for hatchets, scissors, knives, paper, looking glasses, &c.' (Turnbull 1813: 264). The fact that certain islanders travelled with the ship and visited other parts of Polynesia is also noted. These observations clearly are not ethnographic facts of any recognizable kind, and isolated reports are of limited significance in themselves. But only the totality of such fragments can reveal the fundamental changes brought about by barter and make sense of the efforts of certain islanders to emulate mythologized versions of Polynesian histories on other islands (Thomas 1986a: 13). In the same way, a missionary's note that 1,522 lb. of arrowroot was collected (to be exported and sold for the mission) from a district in Samoa says nothing about customs or social structure but does bear upon changes in production and the apparent perpetuation of old competitive displays under a new missionary regime – 'the plan was for each village and town to come separately and in order; we received their parcels of arrowroot' (Slayter 1843: 54).

If these events are as important as I have maintained, then anthropological practice should be different. The ethnographic experience and the statements of a man or woman may have the feel of truth, the sense of 'direct knowledge' of a society or culture. Needless to say, representations of social or cultural attributes are abstractions arrived at through analytical work, and are no more visible than the unconscious. Moreover, the data drawn into the picture arise from the structured experience of the ethnographer, and, if elicited, may take a form (even prior to their representation by the analyst) which they would never take in his or her absence. Still, next to this immediacy, the interpretation of passages in old handwriting or out-of-print books, peppered with pious judgements or racist allusions, may seem hopelessly distant from a living system. These words may, however, reflect the absent causes in the living group: happenings which shape practice or arrangements, but which are not known or spoken of. This implies an anthropological reading of phenomena which are scattered and dispersed outside the bounds of strictly anthropological concerns, a reading of incidents, accidents and misunderstandings – but these turn out to be more systemic than the marginal, residual constitution of events and change beyond the systems envisaged in conventional paradigms would permit one to expect.

Some of the perpetrators of pious reflection and racial stereotyping, or of the events which disrupted 'our' object, the traditional system, ventured to write ethnography before its time. These treatises somehow turn out to be only partly motivated by projects we would eschew; we find that they are frequently structured by a systematizing impulse which is suspicious in what it does to evidence but also suspiciously like our own practice. These discourses might stimulate deeper scrutiny of our own knowledge-project, but are also there to be more innocently read: it is not as though ethnography belongs to the present and history to the past.

7

Evolution of another sort: regional systems theory and the Pacific

What becomes of evolutionary theories under the different intellectual circumstances of contemporary anthropology? Is it in any sense desirable to further elaborate such ideas?

In the fourth and sixth chapters I focussed primarily on the connections between sources, forms of evidence and methods, and interpretations which are mostly seen to be worked out at some distinct level. The fifth chapter aimed to illustrate the argument by sketching out the discrepancy between one theory of Polynesian social evolution and another, based on different forms of evidence and different dealings with the same forms. The point was not epistemological pluralism – the facile observation that a set of facts can sustain diverse interpretations – but rather that the different readings were, to the contrary, partly implicit in methods and the data as constituted. The deeply-seated and salient metaphor of discourse as a building or edifice with 'levels' (especially of abstraction) is particularly pernicious in this context; more apt would be the vision of a tangled forest, in which life-substances are drawn invisibly from above and below, the attributes of an elevated leaf structure having a hidden, conditioning, relationship with the form and content of soil and litter. A secondary forest, of course: all our efforts take place on top of others, constrained yet displacing; the ground impoverished, but perhaps also enriched by fire.

The epistemological argument is not an end in itself. I shift the focus now to the question of the value of an untangled or differently tangled approach to evolution and history – which, although situated in the Pacific, has wider implications, and leads back to more general questions of anthropological practice and epistemology.

The regional systems perspective

One nexus between contemporary anthropology and evolutionism can be traced to the discussions and revisions of Marxist anthropology in the 1970s (see e.g. Bloch 1975; Godelier 1977; Seddon 1978; and the journal *Critique of Anthropology*). These were hardly focussed on evolutionary questions, since such matters as the larger frame of international economic inequalities were of more pressing concern, but nevertheless entailed some critique and reworking of both Marxist evolutionary categories and American neo-evolutionist theory (of the sort developed by Julian Steward [1955] and others). There were debates about modes of production, their (sequential?) associations, the nature of transitions, class formation, and determination in general. The process of modification and reconstruction arguably went so far that by the late seventies the discussion had virtually lost any distinctively Marxist character. In particular, claims that relations of production played a crucial determining role were not sustained. The 'post-Marxist' emphasis on relations which might formerly have been considered superstructural, and on the reproduction of hierarchical structures perhaps therefore ends up having less in common with materialist antecedents than with the sort of exercise attempted by Goldman, which stressed aspects of social organisation and status rather than production.

These trends were perhaps most clearly reflected in a paper by Kajsa Ekholm which was originally published in 1976 (Ekholm 1981; cf. Friedman and Rowlands 1977). One of the key steps is that away from 'stages' or modes of production identified on the basis of local societies towards transformations linking distinct forms, which were understood to arise from the specific properties of systems of appropriation, exchange, and hierarchical reproduction. If, as in earlier approaches, the starting point was the construction of social types such as 'bands', 'chiefdoms', 'early states' or modes of production, transitions between these rigidified forms automatically become problematic. Evolution is detached from the internal properties of society at any particular stage, and is confined to the changes from one form to another. The contrasting concern with connections between the short-term dynamics of a particular form of reproduction and the longer-term dynamics of transformation may bridge the gap between questions about the entities generally observed, namely functioning systems of particular types, and questions about the transition from one type to another. Thus the huge literature about the origin of 'the' state may display an obsession with an issue which would not have seemed as dramatic or inexplicable if processes in a wider variety of hierarchical polities had been taken into account.

The other crucial shift is that away from the single society as the unit of analysis. As Ekholm (especially) stressed, there is a crucial link between this question and the perception of social variation. Two societies, seen as separate cases, may differ dramatically with respect to such traits as the elaboration of elite culture, specialized craft production, political central-ization, and stratification. An evolutionary difference may be read from the presence of these features in one case and their absence in another. However, if in a particular region, such societies are viewed in terms of larger systems

87

of exchange relations, it can be argued that what appears in one case as development or innovation, and in the other as the lack thereof, in fact reflects something like a centre–periphery relation between the two; that is, relations of unequal exchange, together with the centre's monopoly over the widest field of relations, generate the characteristics of 'advanced' or 'backward' groups, which would have no meaning if the framework of relations did not exist. Ideas along these lines have, of course, been extensively discussed by many writers concerned with imperialism and specifically with exposing the notion that the unfavourable position of third-world countries derives from an internal 'underdevelopment' rather than the constraints and impositions of the world system. Such writers have often left the anthropological notion of the more-or-less 'cold' traditional society intact by dealing exclusively with disruption and change consequent upon capitalist penetration. The undesirable and often tragic character of such changes also tends to some idealization of the undisturbed past. The importance of Ekholm's contribution is that it extends an analysis of approximately the same sort back to earlier 'civilizations' (such as Mesopotamia) and to smaller-scale regional systems in general:

On the central plateau of Madagascar a spectacular evolution took place between the end of the eighteenth century and the French occupation at the end of the nineteenth century. As long as the field of inquiry is confined to this region there is nothing which directly contradicts the idea that development is driven by internal forces. Industry and trade expand. A greater area is exploited for irrigated rice, the slave population greatly increases, and developed state and class structures emerge, etc. If, however, the field is broadened to include events in the southeast, the expansion on the plateau becomes more complicated. During the same period the southeast experienced an equally spectacular devolution. Before the expansion on the plateau there were kingdoms and a relatively well developed economy in the southeast. The following evolution on the plateau is accompanied by a successive economic underdevelopment and political fragmentation in the southeast. This simultaneous development and underdevelopment can only be understood by placing Madagascar as a whole in a larger 'global' system in which Western Europe is the major expanding area. The relation between this expansion and the shift in trade patterns on Madagascar (ultimately derivable from the power struggle between France and England in the Indian Ocean) is the fundamental dynamic in the evolution/devolution process.

(Ekholm 1981: 244–5)

It is not important here that Ekholm makes no attempt to substantiate this argument. Our concern is with the theoretical implications of the form of interpretation. The analysis is an 'evolutionary' one in the sense that it is concerned with structural change and development, with transformations linking (comparatively) 'primitive' and 'complex' systems. The discussion is, however, drained of much of the colour and resonance of classic evolutionism. The temporal metaphor which discriminates between societies is disabled: 'earlier' and more 'advanced' forms are represented as outcomes of unitary processes, rather than something like the absence (in the primitive case) of time and growth – which is, of course, ultimately directed towards the elevated specialization and rationality of our own system. A vast amount of popular scholarship has been written along evolutionary lines precisely because evolution has a broader cultural meaning (e.g. Sagan 1985). Goldman's argument was more sophisticated and qualified than those advanced by most nineteenth-century theorists, but even in his work we find social variation subordinated to a logic of increasing stratification. Ekholm's perspective suppresses this directional aspect and thus becomes detached from that specific array of larger ideological meanings, which discriminated in both the neutral and pernicious senses. The symbolic efficacy of evolutionary categories is thus attenuated, but the door is opened for a different kind of talk which perhaps in the end can bear as directly upon a wider interest in the international economy and the struggles and social categories it generates. It would be desirable if one sort of evolutionary discourse informed some undoing of the system which an earlier evolutionary discourse legitimated, but to expect this would undoubtedly be to exaggerate the efficacy of scholarly theorizing.

Obviously the centre–periphery dynamics emphasized by Ekholm do not themselves provide sufficiently specific mechanisms to account for the wider array of local and supra-local processes. The key notion which permits more specific explanation is that of the system of reproduction. This implies some sort of specification of key features which have the effect of reproducing particular hierarchies or social relations, generating developmental processes and cycles, events and longer-term dynamics.

'Prestige-goods systems' in Oceania

The construct of the 'prestige-goods system' illustrates this analysis and, incidentally, exemplifies the general trends in neo-Marxist reformulation alluded to above. The concept was derived from Ekholm's study of the Kongo kingdom of central west Africa and was subsequently generalized in Friedman and Rowlands' model of the evolution of 'civilization' (Ekholm 1977; Friedman and Rowlands 1977: 224–8).

A prestige-goods system is understood as a particular development of the sort of small-scale state which is essentially a federation of graded clans. The basis for dominance changes from genealogical rank to control over foreign exchange, which is very frequently a source of valuables rather than (or as well as) mundane things. The valuable objects, in this system, are not mere expressions of rank, but rather play a crucial role as exchange items, because they are essential elements in important transactions such as marriage exchanges or mortuary ceremonies even at lower rank levels. Their monopolization therefore creates in itself a degree of dependence. The basic hierarchical relationship between a centralizing, monopolizing power and subordinate places entails exchange of tribute against prestige goods. This asymmetrical exchange acquires a larger systemic character outside a strictly 'economic' domain because it is linked with a generalized exchange marriage system, that is, one in which group A gives husbands to B, B gives them to C, and so on. If there is a marriage rule it would amount to matrilateral cross-cousin marriage. Such systems normally have hierarchical content because wife-takers rank higher than wife-givers, but contradictions may arise if the closed nature of the system means that at some point Z must take a wife from A. In prestige-goods systems this problem need not arise, because the highest-ranking group, which is of course also that which monopolizes external trade, can give daughters to its foreign-exchange partners, which may be desirable for political reasons anyway. The overall relationship thus produces a movement of wives and tribute up a hierarchy of groups, in the opposite direction to prestige-goods. The longer-term monopoly may be assured if the prestige-goods are perishable or effectively consumed in some context, such as in burials. These relations, of course, have spatial content: movement 'down' and 'up' the hierarchy entails movement between centres and peripheries. In some cases, such as that described by Ekholm, residence is uxorilocal, meaning that higher-ranking men move from the aristocratic centres to subordinate places (which may effect political control). These relations, according to Friedman and Rowlands, therefore tend to create a pattern of (cultural?) oppositions: higher-ranking men/ lower-ranking women, nobles/commoners, invaders/indigenous inhabitants, etc. (1977: 226). Some of these features persist after the system is transformed into something else, and the argument may help explain the very widespread oppositions in (for instance) parts of west Africa between 'local' commoners and chiefs from outside (e.g. Fortes 1949b). The crucial role of external trade may also lead to a dual chieftainship separating religious and secular (executive) functions.

Friedman applied these ideas to the Pacific in an article entitled 'Notes on structure and history in Oceania' (1981). The argument was essentially that early Austronesian societies ancestral to Melanesian and Polynesian systems – that is, those existing in Melanesia about 4,000 years ago – were prestige-goods systems, and that the historical distribution of social forms in the region reflects various transformations of this original system. The evidence for the early system was essentially that (a) kin terminology reconstructed through historical linguistics indicated generalized exchange and dualism, and (b) long-distance trade was suggested by the distribution of traceable obsidian items in early Melanesian Lapita sites.

Friedman suggested that the overall trend in Melanesia was towards an increase in 'trade density' and more specialized, short-distance trade. This was in part a correlate of increasingly dense settlement, and in particular the settlement of upland areas, which took place in the course of the region's prehistory. The increase in density led, Friedman suggested, to a breakdown of former monopolies over trade and consequently of hierarchy. The result is the pattern of competitive, relatively egalitarian 'big-man' systems so much discussed in Melanesian anthropology. In a few areas, such as the Trobriands and New Caledonia, trade monopoly, chieftainship, and other elements of prestige-goods systems persisted or subsequently re-emerged.

Friedman has relatively little to say either about southern Vanuatu or Fiji, both areas in which documented hierarchical structures rest uneasily with the prestige-goods model, but claims that in western Polynesia, 'full-blown' prestige-goods systems existed. Certainly, there is evidence that Fiji, Samoa and Tonga were involved in a regional exchange system which linked up with internal hierarchies; that spouses and prestige objects such as red feathers (to be woven into mats) were central to these larger relations; that internally tribute was exchanged against valuables; that chiefs attempted to create and maintain monopolies; and that, particularly in Tonga, sacred/secular distinctions emerged in paramount chiefly titles (Kaeppler 1978; Hjarno 1979/80; Gunson 1979).

In eastern Polynesia, on the other hand, it is suggested that a sort of inversion of the Melanesian process took place: external exchange became less significant not because of an increase in the density of trade networks, but because increasing distances between islands made trade impossible. Friedman's suggestion is that the basis of political dominance then shifted to a sort of religious despotism manifested in a great elaboration of prohibitions (*tapu* restrictions) connected with chiefly status. The loss of trade monopoly supposedly led also to greater competition between chiefs, reflected in agricultural intensification and greater mobilisation of surpluses (which were directed into potlach-style feasting). On Tahiti and Hawaii chiefly efforts to unify polities were relatively successful, while in many other cases (Marquesas, Easter Island, Mangaia) intensification allegedly failed, producing a decline in hierarchy, instability, famine, and intense but unresolvable competition.

Although condensed and somewhat insensitive to the intricacies of the evidence, Friedman's argument represents a significant advance upon Goldman's theory. Although his reasons for stressing the contrasts between eastern and western Polynesia turn out to be questionable, Friedman's model does attempt to explain a whole pattern of systematic difference which was acknowledged but passed over by Goldman's account. The integration of Polynesian transformations with Melanesian processes is also an important step, given the recognition which has developed that these major cultural regions not only merge but were linked by processes of settlement and linguistic diversification (Golson 1971; Green 1979; Kirch 1984: 44–48; Pawley 1981). Some of the main contrasts between them turn out to be aspects of explorers' representations and anthropological models rather than social realities.

The subordination of variation to a teleology of increasing centralization, stratification and eventual class formation, in which Hawaii or Tonga is seen as the apex of Polynesian development, is rejected by Friedman. The argument is rather that features of systems of social reproduction in a certain ancestral type give rise to an array of 'descendent' societies under differing historical and ecological conditions. This is not to assume that each society follows an isolated, divergent path of local development once it has separated from other groups; continuing contact, regional relations, and certain kinds of pre-capitalist 'dependent development' may be variously important, but all can be integrated into an account of structural transformation. Evolution is not a principle to be played off against others (such as diffusion).[1]

In broader terms the approach depends upon constructing an ancestral society, a systemic starting point, from which subsequent variations are derived. The subsequent pattern is typically what is found across space at a particular time. A complex of ethnographic diversity can thus be rendered as the mutations of a structure or set of structures. The exercise differs from a more conventional kind of comparison within regions, which simply notes patterns of covariation, perhaps linked with a functional argument about associations between particular elements, which suppose at least implicitly some unspecified kind of synchronic transformation. However, the sort of exercise attempted by Friedman could tend to collapse into something more reminiscent of the earlier style of analysis, because it is difficult to sustain the necessary historical and evolutionary content which differentiates an argument about structural change from the mere rendering of contrasts and differences in terms of temporal or processual metaphors. This is simply to say that there may be gaps between the theory enunciated and that worked out in practice.

In fact, there turn out to be theoretical as well as more empirical problems with Friedman's analysis. Like Goldman, he reproduces the classic evolutionist fallacy of treating (contemporary) society A as an earlier stage of society B. The distinction in the case of Goldman's work was that the logic was disconnected from any possible sequence of historical settlement and development. In Friedman's view, both the regions of earlier and latest settlement – Melanesia and eastern Polynesia – underwent transformation, but the west Polynesian societies in the middle are explicitly understood as the perpetuation of earlier prestige-goods systems: 'the old prestige-good system is preserved until quite late' (1981: 292); while eastern Polynesia is read effectively as the transformation of eighteenth- and nineteenth-century western forms, which 'broke down very early' (*ibid*: 287; cf. 1985: 200–1). Apart from general objections to the notion that hierarchical systems which were obviously fluid should not have changed structurally over some 2,000 years, this suggestion of continuity in Samoa and Tonga (and also eastern Fiji?) is problematic on historical and archaeological grounds.[2]

The notion that the prestige-goods systems broke down in the east because of the quantum increase in distances between island groups seems entirely reasonable when one glances at a map of the Pacific: it is clear that, in the west, the islands are large and relatively close together, and one can envisage frequent contact which would seem impossible in the vast space between the dots in the more profoundly insular environment of eastern Polynesia. The problem with this observation is that it ignores that fact that most of the eastern Polynesian islands are in *groups*, within which distances are often short, and within which regular trade (as opposed to occasional, accidental drift) was feasible. Although the evidence for such exchange makes it difficult to establish its social importance, there is no doubt that it took place. In the Marquesas trade linking southern and northern parts of the group involved movements of parrot feathers, adze stone, processed turmeric, kava, and no doubt other things. Because the primary social groups were *mata'eina'a* or 'tribes' which normally inhabited one valley, this trade did constitute a form of external exchange which could theoretically have been monopolized.

There is abundant evidence for contact and barter between Tahiti and certain other islands. Apart from the frequent contact and politico-religious connections with the windward group of the Society Islands (Huahine, Raiatea and Borabora), there were links more dedicated to exchange with smaller and more peripheral islands such as Me'etia in the east, and via that island (as well as perhaps more directly) with the Tuamotu archipelago (Oliver 1974, I: 213–4). Being atolls, the Tuamotus were strong in pearls and pearl shell, but lacked certain foodstuffs and other 'high island' resources such as volcanic stone for adze blades; their inhabitants thus had basic reasons for maintaining a trade which served more elite concerns in Tahiti. Since the *Bounty* mutineer Morrison specifically noted that the contact between Me'etia and Tahiti was run by the chief of the Taiarapu district (in the island's eastern peninsula, Tahitit Iti) (1935: 201), there is evidence not merely for the possibility of a prestige-goods system but for the monopolization of certain external exchange links which draw in valuables. Yet it is clear that this control was not crucial politically, and that both the reproduction of hierarchy in a systemic sense and more immediate political jockeying depended primarily on things other than the manipulation of trade.

External exchange certainly did become impossible in a few cases, such as Easter Island and Rapa – islands so isolated that it is remarkable that they were settled at all. In other parts of the Austral group (to the south and south-west of Tahiti), and Mangareva, the substantial distances appear to have made contact much more restricted than it was in the Societies and Tuamotus. It is notable, however, that historical processes on Rapanui, in the Marquesas, and on Mangareva, appear to have been broadly similar. In each case (but to a varying degree) the pattern of changes noted in chapter 5 took place: there were shifts in power away from chiefs and towards landholders or warriors, and certain changes in religion (toward more 'inspired' activity). These were least marked in Mangareva and most extreme on Easter Island. The results of broadly similar ecological processes are also apparent: upland forests were lost, consequent erosion narrowed the resource base; in some cases innovative modes of intensive production (such as the cultivation of breadfruit in the Marquesas) were developed. Some of the islands upon which these processes took place are extremely isolated, and others are in island groups, but the possibility of supra-local contact and exchange was evidently not crucial.

These points imply that external exchange is given too much weight in Friedman's model. His view is certainly that its presence, absence, or density produces divergent systems, given that the starting point is a prestige-goods system. Yet it is especially clear from the Tahitian evidence that certain preconditions for a prestige-goods system may exist without such a system in fact developing. The bases of hierarchical reproduction in eastern Polynesia are not absolutely clear, but there is no doubt that control of exchange was not a significant factor before interaction with European traders. It may be the case that 'theocratic feudalism' sometimes does emerge when a prestige-goods system is extended or transported to an area where external exchange is impossible, but this argument is of no relevance to the Polynesian situation, because such a system could in fact have existed in parts of eastern Polynesia. It is, in any case, necessary to reject the supposition that the western Polynesian societies were in fact prestige-goods systems 2,000 years ago, when the colonizing move into eastern Polynesia probably took place: a range of archaeological and traditional evidence indicates that the regional integration upon which the eighteenth-century system depended was in fact a much more recent development (Davidson 1977, 1978; Kirch 1984).

The question then arises of the conditions which promote the development of hierarchical reproduction on the basis of external connections and monopoly rather than tributary transactions in kind, control of religion and the means of production, and so on. Since, in Friedman's explanation, the prestige-goods system is the starting point, it is not in itself explained: there is no theory of where such a system comes from, or of the circumstances under which a hierarchical polity should take that particular turn. Given that explanations have to start somewhere, with a society in history, this is in general a legitimate procedure, but ceases to be so in this case if the historical discontinuity between the western Polynesian societies observed in the late eighteenth century and the ancestral system is recognized: the prestige-goods system becomes another late development which a model of transformations must account for.

Theoretical implications

An earlier section of my argument could be recapitulated (or reinvented) as follows: the anthropological object has always been a social or cultural unity. The understandings of what constitutes this system (or structure) were and are extremely diverse, but a general feature has been that the systemic character of the domain has been erected and sustained in opposition to events and history. The most general form of analysis predicates a part/whole relation in the sense that the significance (and explanation) of a ritual or institution arises from its functional or meaningful coherence in a totality. The work of analysis demonstrates the connection by revealing the context or larger meaning of what is initially singular or puzzling. Past events are understood almost as random or arbitrary, and take place outside the system. This exclusion was initially justified on the basis of the unknowable character of prehistoric contacts between (or changes within) non-literate societies, but was extended to the events of European contact or colonial histories in areas such as (parts of) Africa and the Pacific where there were sharp gaps between the pre-European traditional past and documented erosions or transformations of traditional cultures. No such sharp break existed in most Asian contexts, but the complexities of history were seen as injecting richness and diversity without in any sense having a processual or systemic character which might have been linked with matters closer to the heart of anthropological analysis.

'History' or 'a historical perspective' can apparently be added to or discussed at the same time as 'culture' and 'the social system' but in fact no serious integration is possible unless the exclusions which constitute the latter objects are broken down.

A model which has as its central concern the transformation of 'global' or regional systems of reproduction breaks from more conventional anthropological approaches in a number of ways. It is not alone in insisting upon a supra-local vision, in demanding that attention be paid to larger economic entanglements, but is perhaps exceptional in its emphasis upon the significance of such larger connections in pre-colonial or pre-capitalist contexts. The perspective thus further erodes the dichotomies associated with 'us' and 'them', whereby the west, or some category of civilized or 'hot' societies, exists in history and is subject to constant transformation, while other systems are not constituted historically in the same way. At one level, this opposition is discredited, but is sustained implicitly in anthropological practice in the division of theoretical approaches: crudely, Europe is analysed historically, the 'third-world' and peasant societies are placed in their historical and international economic context, but tribals are somehow particularly amenable to symbolic analysis which passes over such dynamics and processes. The conceptual reorientation thus has ideological implications: it assists in the complicated job of extricating anthropology from playful but pernicious representations of 'others' as inversions or origins of our modernity.

For anthropological theory, it is more significant that transformations are situated at the core of the analysis and are directly linked with the properties of the social system. If changes and short-term fluctuations incorporate or equate with history and events, then what were antithetical in former understandings are now rendered indissociable. There have been many revisions and departures in recent anthropology, but this break – if effectively expressed in analysis – would be crucial, because it bears upon, and causes a shift in, the constitution of the discipline's objects. Something like 'systemic history' is substituted for 'system' (of whatever sort).

The theoretical programme implied by regional systems theory equally has implications for the practice of historical analysis: it does not simply incorporate an existing methodology and link it with a set of concepts. The form of contextualization which most historical writing employs is still the situating of events and circumstances in chronological narrative, although this master-context is partially subordinated to thematic concerns (such as class analysis, gender, popular culture and so on). Discussions of the systemic ramifications or characteristics of events thus tend to be marginal to the story or account, and a matter of tentative generalization rather than contextualization. (There are of course many exceptions, such as works which attempt to construct a system and trace its development through historical processes [e.g. Ste. Croix 1981].) Although reviewing historical analysis in any extensive way is beyond the scope of this study, it can be said that just as a theory of social transformations redefines the anthropological context, it substitutes structured historical processes and dynamics for narrative.

Regional systems in colonial history

These radical implications of the regional systems model emerge in the specific context of the examination of processes consequent upon the engagement of 'traditional' hierarchical systems with the expanding west. As was noted above, the discussion of such changes in contemporary anthropology constituted the residual object of 'social change', generally seen as an unsystematic sequence of loosely connected happenings (the intrusion of Christian missions, changes in work, introduction of cash, etc.). Explanations in this domain were typically weaker and more particular than those concerned with elements of the system proper.

On the other hand, the transformations which figure in a regional systems model can have immediate causes which are either internal or external, and (so far as the latter are concerned) can arise either from interaction with similar regional systems or colonizing powers. There is no overriding distinction between causes which are intrinsic to the anthropological object, and those which stem from what are construed as intrusions or irruptions. As has already been explained, Ekholm's model of the prestige-goods system focusses on the control of external exchange. Having described the functioning of the system in the Kongo case, Ekholm moves on to raise the question of what takes place if prestige-goods are introduced from a new source. This supposes a situation in which some external agent has an interest in what can be obtained in exchange for valuables, which may themselves be novelties (such as manufactured western articles) or may replicate prestige-goods with an established value in the area. If, in either case, the new supply is monopolized by the group which already has the status of a centralizing power in the region, then an initial effect will be that their former external exchange partners will either be excluded or fall into a subordinate position (Ekholm 1977: 130–1). Thus where a central group A traded with B and succeeded in dominating c, d, and e on the basis of exchange monopoly, the novel access to certain goods enjoyed by A will tend to reduce B to the status of the other groups. This is at least what happened in the Kongo case. However, there may often be no reason for the foreign merchant to favour one group within the particular peripheral region, and such factors as uneven exchange rates may favour an array of contacts. If this takes place, the position of A is likely to break down as formerly subordinate groups acquire independent access to valuables. The same dynamic may well take place under various circumstances in the absence of western trade involvement. In the Kongo case, the first phase, of the kingdom's externally stimulated expansion, was relatively brief: but during the sixteenth and seventeenth centuries a long 'devolutionary' process took place, the outcome of which was extreme political fragmentation (*ibid*).

This argument is specific to the Kongo case, and Ekholm does not attempt to map out other possible developments under different circumstances. However, it might be noted that if extensive contacts took place between European traders and peripheral parts of the prestige-goods system, it is likely that the initial phase of political expansion would not take place, unless the central power had some basis for control beyond trade monopoly. If political or military factors facilitated more secure dominance, it is possible that monopoly and the larger polity might have been sustained for much longer. These divergent outcomes would not be the products of unsystematic contingencies, but would rather reflect properties of slightly distinct systems. In this model, an event such as an altered tribute presentation or a war about sovereignty is not simply a happening in a bewildering sequence of happenings, but instead is read as an expression or instantiation of systemic transformation. This view, of course, has implications for methods of research, since the 'contingencies' left aside in other anthropological perspectives assume this distinct importance.

In the context of his discussion of the contacts between eastern and western Polynesia, Friedman alluded in passing to the relevance of this line of argument to the Oceanic case:

In West Polynesia, Europeans encounter a Tongan society without arms or fortified settlements as in East Polynesia. Here, the relatively peaceful Tongan hegemony immediately disintegrates into civil war as the result of European trade. This is the kind of disintegration that Ekholm has shown to be systematic in the contact between hierarchical prestige-good systems and decentralized commercial trade...In East Polynesia, on the other hand, the differential trade in arms and the establishment of alliances with particular chiefs, leads to Western-backed state formation.

(1981: 289–90)

It is in fact the case that the Tongan polity was stable until just after a sequence of visits by Cook, Bougainville and others, but the link between European contact and unprecedented aristocratic conflict is by no means clear. It should be noted that there is much more of a contrast between the Tongan and Kongo cases of collapse than Friedman acknowledges, since although the Tongan hierarchy was ultimately reshaped, its initial breakdown was extraordinarily rapid. It would have to be supposed that a few explorers' visits, which did distribute objects to be partly assimilated into existing categories of valuables, but which certainly conducted no large-scale trade, had the same effect as decades of systematic commercial exchange in the African case. This view would be supported by the fact that the visits of the explorers were distributed around the Tongan group, which might have undermined monopoly, but the absence of evidence for any conflict specifically concerned with the control of external trade is problematic.

The implication so far as eastern Polynesia is concerned is that the prior military orientation of the so-called 'theocratic feudal' form makes great consolidation and expansion on the basis of European support possible. The features of some of the emergent systems in the Society Islands, the Marquesas, and Hawaii are somewhat incompatible with a model of straightforward expansion by conquest, and are curiously reminiscent of features of the prestige-goods system. Chiefs were certainly preoccupied with obtaining European weapons, and the narratives and logs of whalers, traders and other voyagers are full of indications of the intense rivalries which developed between chiefs with respect to European connections. If, however, the uses made of guns are examined, it is clear that obvious military purposes were less important than prestigious display and, most crucially, exchange value. Chiefs who had the opportunity seem to have attempted to create networks of dependence on the basis of their monopoly over supplies of weapons. This was an effective short-term basis for dominance because guns, like traditional prestige valuables, ranked higher than local produce (in the same sense that gold ranks higher than silver or tin), which as tribute might be directly or indirectly exchanged for weapons and other items of European provenance such as beads and cloth. There was thus the possibility of generating indebtedness among subjects, at the same time as tributary obligations were extended. The strategy could not have been sustained in the longer term because it was not systematically linked with other bases for social asymmetry (such as marriage alliances of the kind described by Ekholm) and because chiefs who created indebtedness by distributing weapons also simultaneously undermined their own security. The connections between the varying nature of the indigenous systems and post-contact histories emerge in the degree to which chiefly attempts towards expansion were successful. The contrast between the faltering and fractured character of polity and chiefly expansion in the Marquesas and consolidation in Hawaii and the Society Islands clearly has much to do with the virtual absence of centralizing tributary appropriation in the former case and the strength of such mechanisms in the latter groups.

But as one moves later into the nineteenth century it becomes increasingly apparent that the argument linking pre-contact systems of reproduction and the array of colonial histories has a long way to go in the Oceanic case. There are striking differences between the colonial histories of eastern and western Polynesia, but if the whole of the nineteenth century is taken into account, they are not the contrasts the prestige-goods model would predict. Friedman's suggestion that the navigators' intrusion produced instability in the Tongan case may turn out to be correct, but the outcome of the longer-term process of interaction was a consolidated indigenous monarchy – in fact the only one in the Pacific which escaped any phase of formal colonial control (cf. Latukefu 1970).[3] In both Tonga and Samoa, transformed versions of traditional chiefly hierarchies have continued to be important right up to the present, and the involvement of members of traditional chiefly families in government is still notable in the whole west Polynesian region. While the original basis for hierarchy in the control of prestige-goods may thus have broken down at an early date, there is no comparison between this region and a case such as Kongo, where a kingdom vanished into a mass of localized, egalitarian societies.

In eastern Polynesia, the polities apparently based on tributary appropriation and predatory military action tended to expand rapidly if unevenly, but broke down after a few decades. Thus the systems which might have been expected to be stronger than those based on exchange were in fact less effective in accommodating or resisting colonial encroachment. Most east Polynesian aristocratic structures were of much diminished significance by the 1850s, and today – in sharp contrast with western Polynesia – it is very difficult even to identify families with chiefly backgrounds. Such links, where known, are socially insignificant.

An account of these processes must, of course, incorporate variation in the nature of colonial entanglements and intrusions. At a crude level it could be observed that settlers and officials in eastern Polynesia actively attempted to obtain control of land and impose administrations of some sort in place of indigenous arrangements. This was most true of Hawaii, where the reorganization of land (in 1848) and the expansion of the sugar industry virtually proletarianized a substantial proportion of the indigenous Hawaiian population (although most of the actual plantation workers were recruited from China) (Kent 1983: 35f.). In French Polynesia there was no comparable large-scale dispossession, but missions and officials pushed both the Tahitian monarchs and many lesser chiefs aside. On Easter Island the impact of the Peruvian slave raid of 1862 was so extreme that it is hardly worth mentioning subsequent injustices before and after the Chilean annexation – although it should be known that this sorry history is apparently soon to be compounded by the construction of a US space shuttle base on the small island (IWGIA 1987: 31).

The appropriate contrast in the later history is between Hawaii and Fiji. The British colonial effort in the latter case amounts to a classic instance of indirect rule, and although this certainly had oppressive features which neither the officials nor the various groups of complicit chiefs acknowledged, the efforts of capitalist planters to alienate land were largely frustrated by an administration committed to the perpetuation of Fijian rights. The communal system persisted not so much because the government had an enlightened recognition of how limited the benefits of development were, but because the official promotion of more individualistic and competitive economic practices was in general successfully resisted or passively obstructed by Fijians (Macnaught 1982). The crucial precondition for this significant if partial degree of autonomy was the retention of the land. Explanations must therefore incorporate the systematic character of intrusions and their diverse forms.

These considerations only qualify the extent to which features of post-contact change and colonial history can be regarded as effects of the dynamics of pre-contact systems. The question is to some extent simply one of time-scales, since the burden of the past is altered as an immediate past recedes. In later phases of colonial history the properties and strategies of the colonizing system seem to overshadow those of that which is colonized. To acknowledge this is only to recognize the profound asymmetries of determination which give colonial and neo-colonial processes their character. An effective model must accommodate both structured histories. The challenge is to compound the time-scales and reveal the working-out of structures generated in one place and time at another; to expose the interpenetration of what might be called the recent and (to play on ambiguity) the historic; that is, the system of contingency. The political pertinence of this in the neo-colonial context arises from the fact that histories of dominance, and of the origins of the problems which bedevil administrations, are always ideologically significant: accidents and the outcomes of structure are talked about differently, blamed, made into precedents, and otherwise manipulated. Efforts to clarify or demystify tend to be of value to at least some of the people involved.

8

Histories structured and unstructured

An abundance of recent writing suggests that the absence of history or time has become, in contemporary anthropology, a critical lack: it is seen almost as an injury which demands immediate attention. The work of dealing with a formerly suppressed dimension, of rectifying an omission, or noticing a forgotten cause, may be seen as a straightforward project, sufficient in itself. The constitution of truth is after all seen as an arithmetic matter – a 'narrow' perspective can only facilitate a partial vision, while the 'adding' of further perspectives produces something fuller, a more complete appreciation. I have already attempted to destabilize these metaphors by suggesting that some perspectives cannot be simply 'added' to others, since their objects are incompatible, demanding disjunct exclusions.

In this chapter I turn in another direction to scrutinize what sorts of 'time' and 'history' might be the object of incorporation. It is obvious that there are distinct if largely implicit concepts of time which have quite divergent analytical implications. Consider for example Bourdieu's critique of the structuralist understanding of gift exchange, which insists that the reality of the act has everything to do with its temporality, with judgements of haste or delay.

It is all a question of style, which means in this case timing and choice of occasion, for the same act – giving, giving in return, offering one's services, paying a visit, etc. – can have completely different meanings at different times, coming as it may at the right or wrong moment... (1977: 6)

The time which is asserted here is clearly the time of experience, of forseeable futures, of memories and lived expectations. It is not the same as the longer run which sees forms of gift-giving or larger exchange relations change. The aim is to install time in things which might be said to happen all the time; that is, stereotypic, described events. Such 'events' are, like institutions and relations, part of the total set of seeming possibilities which constitute a general image of social life. Visiting and offering one's services are perpetually 'on the cards': it is the temporal structure of card-playing which we are drawn towards here, and it is somehow obvious that this should be the case.

102

Why raise questions about the players' biographies, or the history of the situation of play?

There are thus ways of integrating time which integrate one time-scale to the exclusion of others,[1] which therefore say nothing about – for instance – the changes arising from metropolitan intrusions in a studied place, that is, from the historic entanglements with larger systems which make observation possible. On the other hand, other scales, such as the longer time of prehistoric social evolution, and the political histories of centuries, will fail to specify experiential immediacies, the constituents of lived change. We thus confront questions of the implications of privileging certain time-scales and must then make judgements about the sort of talk we favour – since it is illusory to suppose that all understandings might be condensed in some larger, embracing framework.

Both structuralism and functionalism are oriented primarily towards domains which are constituted as 'synchronic': what falls within the space, or along the line, of diachrony is, as has been noted above, an unsystematic residue, which is not exactly amenable to rigorous analysis. The sort of approach which can break out of these terms suppresses the dichotomy by constituting the system in (diachronic) processes. This is the potential – at least at a theoretical level – of regional systems theory. This promise might however underline the separation between studies of systems and studies of change, since that perspective has dealt primarily with larger shifts in exchange systems, with the explanation of patterns of intensification and development, and with the erosion and consolidation of hierarchy. It has thus had only a tangential bearing on the area of cultural analysis, which is central to the concerns of anthropologists.

Structures in time

The attempt to integrate history and the analysis of cultural structures in the recent work of Marshall Sahlins is therefore of considerable interest here. This is so specifically because Sahlins moves from the mere observation that cultural notions and structures are enacted, and therefore exist in time and practice, to the point that action in the world is often at odds with expectations and received categories. A cultural system generates action and orders events, but cannot entirely encompass what takes place. This discrepancy is the source of cultural revaluation and shifts in meanings. This is meant to be true whether one is speaking of the 'dialectic of sense and reference' in the routine existences of social beings anywhere, or of the profound and apparently abrupt changes which mark the encounters between the West and various non-western Others. The arguments depend particularly on a history which has been mythologized as much by Europeans as by Polynesians – the events associated with Cook's visit and death in

103

Hawaii in 1778–79. The analysis is significant also because it considers changes which took place in the earliest phases of contact between an indigenous people and Europeans, which has implications for any attempts to 'reconstruct' pre-contact societies and cultures.

It is well known that tribal peoples who have had limited contact with whites or outsiders frequently believe initially that Europeans are returned ancestors or gods. Anthropologists generally have little to say about such constructions, perhaps simply because the ideas involved seem uncomplicated or uninteresting, but perhaps also because the relativist impulse is to downplay confusions which seem to bring out the credulity of people whose modes of thought we wish to depict as different but no less rational than our own. Yet it would be surprising if a concrete identification between an ancestor and a living intruder did not lead to some reformation of ideas about what ancestors are – a question which of course might be at the heart of an investigation of 'traditional' religion.

The Hawaiians' identification of Captain Cook with their god Lono amounts to a special example of this broader phenomenon, deriving its significance partly from the fact that both the stranger populations and the Hawaiian pantheon were hierarchically differentiated. One can envisage that under these circumstances it is possible for the highest-ranking stranger to be recognized as a supreme deity, who presumably embodies crucial powers. The case reveals that if a white foreigner is treated as a particular god, rather than simply as some divine being, then the cultural categories which relate that god to others and to effects in the world, must change. And since cosmologies are not composed of discrete equations, the ramifications of one conceptual shift necessarily affect other sets of signs.

One of the premises of Sahlins' study is effectively that we do not initially know who Cook was. Facts such as his date and place of birth, his training, and the indisputably impressive list of the places he charted constitute the biographical knowledge that schoolchildren in Australia and New Zealand are somehow thought to need, but this sequence of located achievements adding up to a heroic career was obviously not the Hawaiians' Cook. Sahlins' attempt to know Cook proceeds by way of a sketch of the figures and agents of Hawaiian political cosmology.

There was a fundamental opposition between a usurping warrior chiefship and a generative, indigenous sponsor of agricultural fertility and general well-being. The former was identified with Ku, the god of war, and a large number of particular gods conceived as species or bodies of Ku, and was reflected in myths of invading chiefs from distant lands who killed or expelled local chiefs and priests and who instituted a new religion in which human sacrifice figured prominently. Ku was closely associated with the Hawaiian kings, but was displaced over a four-month period of regenerative winter rain, when the image of Lono toured the island, receiving offerings and giving new life to gardens. During this annual Makahiki festival it was as though the order prior to usurpation regained ascendancy: all the ceremonies associated with Ku were suspended, and the king was secluded. As the period ended, Lono was displaced and the king incorporated or appropriated his powers. The antagonism between the two was manifested in a sham battle at a late stage in the annual ritual (1981: 10–17; cf. 1985b: 206f.; Valeri 1985).

All this is significant because, in Sahlins' version, the pervasive mode in Polynesian thought was recapitulation: the definite struggles between chiefs in traditional history are prefigured in more abstract cosmological oppositions, while the legends themselves generate the understanding and acts of nineteenth-century personae. Biography thus reproduces myth and cosmology. While the Polynesians constructed their own identities in these terms, more or less unwitting foreigners tended to get caught up in this scheme also. There was a sort of logic of assimilation of persons just as there was with things: European hatchets and alcohol were incorporated into indigenous categories of objects, and thus carried the meanings and potential uses of prior classes of things (cf. Thomas n.d.1; Baré 1985: 178–9).

It might be thought that Cook's foreignness would make an identification with Ku-type gods likely, and the suggestion that he was offered and accepted indigenous women would have marked this sort of usurpation. However, the timing of his visit, and his circuit of the island, fitted all too neatly with the Makahiki circuit of the Lono image, and he was identified with that god. Cook was addressed as Lono, and was prepared to go through various ceremonies and receive offerings. The coincidences were compounded when Cook's ships left at about the right time, the officers reassuring the Hawaiian priests that they would return the following year. In asserting that Cook was a myth before he was an event, Sahlins thus identifies Cook as a particular, novel form of the deity. By leaving at the appropriate time, he submitted to the authority of the ruling chief in the same way as Lono's powers were annually subordinated. While this was consistent with the traditional Hawaiian scheme, Cook's ship came back far too soon: one of the masts was damaged, and the expedition returned only days after leaving. Cook as Lono now posed a more definite threat to the regime of Ku and the ruling chief. Relations with the Hawaiians deteriorated, and there was a number of incidents of theft and violence, culminating, of course, in Cook's death on 14 January 1779. Although this was not premeditated, it was consistent with the Hawaiian scheme: Lono was vanquished and his *mana* incorporated by the victor. Britishness in names and things subsequently became a key symbol of the incorporation of this foreign power among the Hawaiian chiefs. The emphasis here is on the recapitulation of structure, of novel content in reproduced forms.

An important feature of Sahlins' argument is, however, the subsequent transformation of Hawaiian categories through their encounter with new

105

events and situations. In the decades following Cook's death, trading relations between Hawaiians and Europeans intensified, meeting a European demand for sandalwood and provisions, and Hawaiian demands for iron, fabric, beads, axes, guns, and many other things. Hawaiian chiefs sought to control the movements of these prestigious things through extensions of the *kapu* (the Hawaiian form of *tapu*) system, inventing various restrictions to facilitate monopoly, but thereby altering the meanings of *kapu*. On the other hand, the involvement of sailors with common women made it possible for the women to violate *kapu* such as those connected with eating meat, or eating with men, which their common menfolk were complicit in because they wanted the objects received in exchange for sexual services. Thus while the primary categorical opposition in pre-European Hawaiian culture was between male and female, which roughly accorded with *kapu*/non-*kapu*, trade created a novel solidarity between common men and women, and a deeper opposition between them and chiefs. These propositions might be disputed, but the general point is clear – that the conjunction of structure and practice brings about a revaluation and reordering of categories.

In *Historical metaphors* as well as in the article 'Structure and history' (in Sahlins 1985a) the general theoretical propositions are stressed. Action takes place in terms of received categories and structures are thereby reproduced. On the other hand, since situations do not necessarily reflect categories, structures may be reordered or transformed in the course of reproduction. The overall distinctions between stability and change, and structure and event, are set up as unhelpful western constructions which obscure the temporality of system on the one hand, and the systemic dimensions of events on the other. The effect of these assertions is to elevate the significance of history and events (since categories are revalued through practice) but also to depict the subsequent encompassment of events by a cultural order. Things in the world may be initially intransigent, but the reordering and modification of sense (at least temporarily) incorporates reference.

In Sahlins' vision, the extent to which cultures tolerate and respond to the necessary discrepancy between the world as constituted and the world experienced is not uniform. He offers a rough contrast between 'prescriptive' and 'performative' cultural structures: in the former case, the orientation is towards conformity with type, or with established traditions: circumstances and events are assimilated to a prevailing order, their perhaps divergent nature being suppressed. On the other hand, 'performative orders assimilate themselves to contingent circumstances' (1985a: xii); they thus extend themselves, renegotiate rules, and invent political forms. They accommodate the disjunction between structure and event which prescriptive forms resist. The Hawaiian system – as one would expect from the analysis – exemplifies a performative order, while Australian Aborigines and apparently also the Maori represent the prescriptive type. In the latter case practice is so intimately linked with cosmological and mythological precedent that Sahlins writes of 'mytho-praxis': 'the Maori past is a vast scheme of life-possibilities'; 'events are hardly unique or new but are immediately perceived in the received order of structure, as identical with their original'; 'the Maori world unfolds as an eternal return, the recurrent manifestation of the same experiences' (1985a: 57–9).[2] We might note here that time tends to collapse into a relationship between the ancestral and the present, the general and the particular. Cosmology is remote and elemental, genealogical myth more recent and specific. The discussion at this point thus deals with time as a distancing element in a cultural structure, rather than a dimension and constituent of more immediate social life.

We might be more concerned by the fact that the process of transformation seems to have got lost hereabouts. Sahlins suggests that prescriptive and performative orders are 'differentially "open" to history' (1985a: xii) but a reader might be forgiven for taking the latter as open and the former as essentially closed. Sahlins acknowledges the connections between this pair of terms and Lévi-Strauss's somewhat notorious opposition between 'hot' and 'cold' societies (Lévi-Strauss 1966: 233–4). Since Lévi-Strauss's observation was strictly about a cultural order rather than any facts of actual change, it can be defended against the charge that history is being denied. But because Sahlins' structuralism might itself be said to be performative, having ostensibly extended itself to incorporate history, the nature of change in these systems would have to be addressed in a more serious way. Despite the fact that Sahlins' theory is partly an account of change, the implication is curiously that prescriptive categories endlessly resist revaluation, events continuing to be received in terms of a prior scheme, even the same prior scheme. It is hard to see how consequential change can occur at all under such a rigorous regime of cultural reproduction. Yet of course we know from archaeology that major transformations in subsistence, settlement patterns, and probably also political organization, did take place in the prehistories of Australia and New Zealand.

The problem stated in these terms is perhaps only acute if Sahlins' concept of the prescriptive system is adopted in an extreme form. But a more significant difficulty of the same kind arises if other aspects of his histories are considered.

What another kind of epistemology might have called the 'test case' for the theory is, of course, that of the Hawaiians' Cook. Here, as Friedman (1985: 191) has noted, the events which structure fails to encompass are those arising from external contact rather than internal transformation. The specific aspects of these circumstances mean that there is a definite source for radical change which is highly restricted and localized, in the sense that the crucial events were all connected more or less directly with the presence of Cook's ships and the interaction of himself and his men with the Hawaiians.

While Sahlins claims that a case of this kind simply brings out processes which are far more general (1981: vii) it is notable that more typical, primarily internal change would entail a dialectic which is both more general and less marked. The conflict between cultural sense and experiential references would be at once more piecemeal and more gradual. What is singular about something like the confrontation between Hawaiians and Englishmen is the source of difference between system and events – because we are offered a Hawaiian system and foreigners' acts (which nevertheless become Hawaiian events). This fertile difference is something quite other than 'the shadow' which routinely falls between 'the idea and the reality' (as in T. S. Eliot's 'The hollow men').

Every relationship subsists in physical or mental acts: assertions, transactions, perceptions, reflections. The moment of instantiation is necessarily, in some minimal sense, a moment of transformation. Every interaction between a couple of friends both newly produces their relationship and redefines it in some way, just as any workers' strike must reproduce class relations while giving them a new meaning. To emphasize the 'indissoluble synthesis' of system and event (Sahlins 1985a: 156) is to stress a profound truth about the dimensions of experience, but it may be mistaken to regard this as the basis of a useful theory of social, cultural or historical change. The problem is that the observation that change is inherent in enactment leads to a theory of history in which there is no source for change apart from the discrepancy between sense and reference.[3] This has spectacular generative potential in the Hawaiian case because the gap between categories and happenings in what might be called the inter-enactment of structures is so considerable. It might also be noted that the particular force of the larger argument derives from the dominant metaphors of recapitulation and genealogy in Polynesian culture: the theory is, as it were, made for the case study. Although experience is frequently modelled in some sense upon narrative, the argument can only be made in a stronger form where this is an explicit process.

In more typical cases the 'indissoluble synthesis' of reproduction and change would assume an almost mechanistic character, as in Bourdieu's formulation of the circular relations between agents' dispositions, strategies and the *habitus* (1977: 78 and *passim*). In general, transformation would be necessary, but minimal: the 'theory' provides no warrant for any sort of social change which differs fundamentally from the sort of gradual linguistic change that takes place through usage – unless one is dealing with particular and dramatic situations of confrontation. A system or cultural structure may therefore necessarily entail change without thereby having a dynamic; it may even have a 'history' (in some narrow sense) without being characterized by any kind of structural transformation or evolution.

This accounts for the fact that the 'events' which the Hawaiian system is

108

shown to deal with are generated by an external system. These events do not themselves amount to any kind of structured history. In so far as the Hawaiian order itself is considered, the old anthropological opposition between a coherent system of some sort, and a disconnected stream of events, is in fact reproduced. The analysis is novel in its depiction of the revaluation of categories arising from these events, but does not depict events and transformations generated within the system itself. We thus have no vision of what change in Hawaii before contact would have been like, beyond limited incremental difference arising through enactment and revaluation. The indigenous system is only historicized in its dealings with Europeans; there is no basis in this historical structuralism for theories of indigenous change or of the major transformations which made Hawaiian, Tahitian and western Polynesian societies into systems which look quite different. The problem is more acute in the Maori case, since the prescriptive form is supposed to constrain even this minimal incremental change.

An objective of any serious theory in social or cultural analysis must presumably be to account for the distinctiveness of particular cases. Although many problems arise in the analysis of the positional significance of local meanings, in determining the form of social relations and dynamics, the intellectual endeavour should not be limited to such concerns. The structuralist analysis of history says something about how schemes of meaning incorporate events and thus takes into account the origins of some elements of the system, but does not go very far in this direction. There is essentially no attempt to deal with longer-term structural transformations, although these are the processes which differentiated the Polynesian societies in the first place. The analysis of history developed by Sahlins and some of his associates is thus a very limited theory, which says nothing about the historical processes which actually make the conditions of life and culture variable across time and space. If analysis is to effectively embrace this wider range of questions, the interpretation of archaeological evidence needs to be linked much more directly with social and historical analysis.

Metaphors in time or temporal metaphors? Sahlins' implicit evolutionism

The grounds for this objection become more substantial if Sahlins' comparison of Hawaiian and Maori culture (1985b) is examined. The argument starts with the point that both groups shared a common central Polynesian cosmology, of which the crucial notion was perhaps that while gods are the sources of life, they do not automatically or willingly facilitate or comply with human needs: 'men are compelled to secure their own existence by inflicting a defeat upon the god, appropriating thus the female power – the bearing earth' (1985b: 197). The thesis is that what is generalized and humanized in the Maori case is 'transposed to the register of kingship'

109

in Hawaii (*ibid*: 196). In the Maori case, divine power is generally appropriated: agricultural fertility ritual is a matter in which everyone participates, re-enacting the conflict between the deities Tu (identified with man) and Rongo (the ancestor of crops). In the Hawaiian case, Ku is identified with the king, who is opposed to, and alternates with, Lono: in the course of the annual Makahiki fertility ritual mentioned above, the god regenerates the land, but is then displaced and defeated by the king. Thus

everything happens as it the agricultural rites of the Maori *hapu* [local group] were expanded in the Hawaiian Makahiki to the totality of society and the generality of the universe. The cosmological exaggeration is corollary to the hierarchical transformation, to the incarnation of the human species in the king.   (*ibid*: 210)

This argument leads to a number of intriguing contrasts, but some of the underlying ideas are deeply problematic. At one level, the description simply exposes a series of differences, either case being represented as a 'version' of the other (e.g. 203, 205–6). However, it is also made quite clear that these contrasts are to be correlated with 'the transformation to divine kingship' (216). There is thus a strong implication that the Maori case is a sort of initial state, which Hawaiian society and culture have developed from. What animates the argument is not simply a pattern of similarity and difference, but connection, movement and inversion: what intrigues us about human sacrifice in Hawaii is not, in this case, its internal features, but the fact that it figures at one point in the shift *from* a metonymic man–god relation in the Maori case – warriors act as gods and reproduce divine struggles in cannibalistic warfare – *to* the 'metaphoric submissions and associations' (215) of the king's sacrifice. This from–to argument draws much of its salience from the assertion that a certain process of social transformation took place, but there is no interest in describing or specifying this process. Despite the emphasis on the connections between structure and change in other areas of Sahlins' work, the links break down in this case: there is no suggestion that particular patterns of change are associated with either form, and any process of transition or evolution is reduced to something which links the types but is basically external to the systemic properties in either case. We thus have an implied position close to the neo-evolutionist analysis of various 'stages' in social development which in fact said very little about transformations between essentially discrete forms.

In the constitution of Maori society as the initial or early form we encounter the same more specific problems as were identified in Goldman's argument. No anthropologist would make an explicit claim that Maori society remained static between some early date when the Hawaiians went off in their own innovative direction and the time of encounters with Cook and other early voyagers. But a claim of precisely this kind is entailed in Goldman's and Sahlins' arguments. Such a view might have a minimal degree of plausibility if the Hawaiian population could be viewed as a branching-off from the Maori, but the prehistory is more complicated (cf. Kirch 1986). Despite the indisputable fact of common origin, the colonizing Maori groups came from the ancestral east Polynesian population at a different time, and, presumably, under different conditions. These questions are in any case secondary if processes of local development and divergence in New Zealand are acknowledged, but such a history is inadmissible if the relationship Sahlins postulates between the Maori and Hawaiian cases is to be sustained.

Structural creativity and individual agency: actors and victims in history

One of the dominant themes in Pacific history since the 1950s has been the agency of islanders. Contrary to the crude images in popular accounts such as Moorehead's *Fatal impact* (1968) of foreigners and particularly missions rapidly and savagely disrupting indigenous cultures, it has been stressed that islanders were never passive dupes or simple victims of Europeans. In this context the evidence for the active manipulation of settlers and missionaries by islanders toward their own ends has been emphasized, as have various internal rationales for participation in relations and transactions which appear exploitative from a western perspective (Davidson 1955; Howe 1984). This theme is of much wider significance, and the question of the extent to which oppressed groups within societies, and in a variety of colonial contexts, have been victims overwhelmed by superior force and circumstances, or actors who played a part in creating their own situation, has been often raised (e.g. Thompson 1963).

With respect to contacts and relations on colonial peripheries, such arguments postulate a certain intransigence on the part of a local culture: outsiders' offerings or demands are accepted in so far as they accord with a prior scheme of aims and strategies. The arguments of Sahlins develop a complementary theme in stressing the creative dynamics of the indigenous cultural scheme. Cultural items, stray things such as names and new objects, are incorporated into an uncompromised order, just as new channels entailing guns or ship-travel come to facilitate old ends. The treatment of Cook as a god reflected symbolic appropriation rather than submission, just as the celebrated aristocratic rejection of the *kapu* system in 1819 reflected earlier moments of political and religious transformation, rather than the abandonment of Hawaiian culture for Christianity. The acquisition of alcohol as 'British kava' similarly arose from the incorporation of Europeanness as a distinct Tahitian political symbol, rather than some corrosive process of 'acculturation' (cf. Thomas n.d.1).

Neither the historians nor Sahlins have acknowledged that these resistant elaborations of local culture entail a particular power relation which could

111

exist only at a certain phase of colonial history, namely the period between initial contact and the establishment of formal metropolitan rule or some form of disruptive occupation. The projection of European power was restrained by lack of interest and constrained by a degree of resistance which tended to be overriden in later phases. The demands of European shipping – which mostly had the means to overcome certain forms of indigenous resistance – were generally limited to what could be obtained through exchange on the periphery of local societies. Certain traders sought commodities such as sandalwood, *bêche-de-mer*, pearls and pork; many visitors simply wanted fresh water and provisions. In neither case was it significant how these goods were obtained: the demands were not linked with any interest in owning land, controlling resources, organizing labour beyond a minimal and temporary degree, or otherwise interfering in internal relations. Attempts were generally made by navigators to determine the forms and terms of barter, but these were often not accepted by islanders, who frequently refused to participate if dissatisfied with what was offered in return for their goods. Although some of these visitors expressed their disapproval of local warfare or such customs as infanticide to the chiefs with whom they dealt, there was no serious effort to alter the indigenous order. Like the north American fur trade, this interaction had all sorts of ramifications, and tended to generate internal dependence on external exchange, but left the indigenous people with a great deal of autonomy.

Missionaries, on the other hand, had the desire but not generally the capacity to restructure indigenous societies. Although many would perhaps have found the notion of displacing chiefs and assuming authority themselves agreeable, and would have had few reservations about imposing a novel social order, this in fact took place on very few occasions (although some missionaries were certainly politically influential). Particularly in earlier phases, missionaries were frequently isolated, relatively impoverished, and were not visibly supported by impressive outside forces. So far from being in a position to disrupt beliefs or proscribe customs, they sometimes had difficulty in obtaining provisions and minimal co-operation. In some later cases, legal codes drawn up by missionaries were adopted in native polities, but these reflect the expansion of certain chiefs' power in the guise of evangelism, rather than the overriding effectiveness of missionary intervention.

Connections with foreigners were thus locally manipulated and willingly reproduced, rather than imposed. There was space under these circumstances for precisely the sorts of innovative meanings discussed by Sahlins. Since foreign links actually tended to be positively valued, the logic of meanings was extended to encompass and in some sense appropriate selected aspects of what was foreign.

The properties of a formal colonial situation in which administrative rule is asserted, or one in which intruders dispossess natives for land or labour, are of course very different. It is one thing to speak of a performative culture order which assimilates itself to contingencies, and quite another for a people to find their leaders powerless, themselves landless, and their crucial ritual practices proscribed. Such people will find the 'working misunderstandings' which sometimes operate so creatively in the inter-enactment of cultural structure do not in fact work. The sort of 'assimilation' Sahlins describes in the Hawaiian case is not as radical as his theoretical discussion would suggest, since cultural forms adapt themselves to novel content. An unexamined power situation is supposed in which agents sustain a set of concerns and objectives not primarily dictated by external influence. A different power situation will displace agents; the salience of the cultural structure which specifies their positional values will evaporate; some other logic must emerge which expresses the novel situation; cultural change will lack the continuity which can be discerned if, at some level, it is terms in a structure which change, rather than a structure's conditions of existence. It is tedious to observe that there is always persistence and change, but the differences in degree do entail types of transformation which are qualitatively distinct.

This is not to say that indigenous cultures are in some simple sense 'destroyed' and replaced by introduced categories, since even in contexts where metropolitan languages have been imposed, where everything seems remote from any traditional past, fundamental notions of personhood and agency are often found which have little to do with those of the dominant culture. But the mechanisms in these cases are quite different: sometimes the dominated people half-adopt the colonizers' representations, even if they invert them and positively assert whatever the dominant culture denigrates. Thus, in what have become 'traditional' communities in parts of modern Hawaii, the virtues of gift-giving, reciprocity and egalitarianism in interaction are stressed, not because such practices really reflect anything that has persisted since former times, but precisely because sharing and parity reverse the rules of the external monetized world, in which such communities are poor and marginal (Linnekin 1984). Sharing and reciprocity have often merely been regarded as typical features of simpler societies, and it has not been noted that what is crucial is often a behavioural ethic which exists in the absence of actual equity and redistribution. It is revealing that in New Guinea it is common for this type of egalitarian sharing to be referred to by a pidgin term, *wanwan* (one-one, to give equally to each); this implies that the ethic derives from such contexts as plantations, where the fraternal solidarity of indigenous workers is asserted against inequality in their external relations with managers (and others such as traders) (Thomas n.d.2). It can be argued

113

that this type of oppositional cultural expression is very widespread in both colonial and non-colonial situations (cf. Beckett 1987: 92, 108–9, *passim*); that, for instance, many of the singular features of hunter-gatherer societies derive not from pristine simplicity but rather from the facts of their 'encapsulation' by threatening and potentially dominant groups dependent on other forms of production. In these situations, historical relations must be constitutive rather than contingent in both the cultural account of local meanings and in any adequate description of social relations.

The Cook/Lono case is thus only a model for a certain class of historical changes. Such processes perhaps took place more in the Pacific than on colonized continents, because the insular nature of Pacific societies provided some defence against disruption, and gave greater space to indigenous manipulation of relatively manageable colonial intrusions. In these cases it can justly be claimed that we see the local incorporation of a constituted 'world system' rather than the integration and subordination of the locality in the global economy. But there came a time in each place – perhaps in a few places it is still to come – when these incursions ceased to be manageable. The histories subsequent to that time cannot be seen in terms of the increments and extensions of an indigenous cultural logic. The stream of outside offerings ceases to be a matter of contingent events which internal structure selectively receives and accommodates, and the structural aspect of what is external itself impinges on the local system and its contingencies.

Culture in history

These critiques demand an extension of anthropological vision in two directions: first, further back in time, into processes which generate social variation and historical dynamics; and second, toward dealing with the array of inter-societal processes, including those constitutive of colonial systems, and their local effects.

Many categories in social analysis entail judgements about relative complexity, inequality, cultural elaboration, productive capacity, and so forth. These situate societies in implicit evolutionary terms but do not acknowledge that processes and even sequences are imputed. The opposition between prescriptive and performative cultural orders is another of this kind, since it is clear enough that we find relatively 'heated' histories in the latter case – which is to say, sequences of change and development more like our own, and less like the repetitive time of real primitives. The contrast between New Zealand and Hawaii implies the evolution from the former to the latter, which we would presume to manifest a more general process.

Larger social categories are essential because certain crude classes do have features in common, including ways of dealing or coping with metropolitan intrusions, but if anthropology is to amount to more than an articulation of the ideology enacted in these instructions, the basis of such types and transformations needs to be specified. Actual history can displace the evolutionary narrative as the necessary chronological structure which encompasses the variety of cases and gives them a more general meaning in our own culture. Where there is no long documentary record, archaeological evidence is a crucial element of this movement of explication, since it pertains to located histories and makes a break from culturally-charged evolutionary schema.

The difficulty is that the bearing of archaeological evidence upon social processes, or upon the social processes which are salient in a particular historical situation, is highly variable. Much of the evidence relates to specific technological matters, rather than subsistence, trade, settlement changes, political organization, and so on. Linking what can be attested to archaeologically with what can be historically documented or ethnographically observed can involve making associations between different timescales. The potential effects of long-term processes which have general effects in intensive or less intensive production, in an orientation toward exchange or warfare, must be linked with historic outcomes among groups of related societies. Diversity at a particular time – some centuries ago, in the early contact period, under colonialism, or in the present – can be the key to the unfolding of short- and long-term transformations. Attempts to 'translate' between prehistory and a new kind of socio-historical inquiry will be problematic or not, depending on whether existing work is compatible with such objectives. In the Pacific, there has always been some co-operation between anthropologists, prehistorians and historians, and there is thus a basis for more integrated projects.

An essential component of any more broadly based investigation is the colonial process. This has a bearing which has mostly been unrecognized upon the terrain of symbolic and interpretive anthropology. The reactive, oppositional character of certain prominent cultural processes simply cannot be understood unless there is some appreciation of wider relations and of the histories through which particular asymmetries arise. This may seem uncontentious, but the fact is that the numerous shifts in the anthropological perspective have preserved the basic idea that what is studied is a system at a particular time. The importance of the colonial context has, of course, been stressed by various writers (e.g. Worsley 1957; Asad 1973), but the effect of this insight has been limited, because the interdependence of theory, methods, and the larger orientation of anthropological discourse has not been recognized. Some theoretical perspectives have emphasized certain kinds of time, but have not often effectively integrated ethnographic facts and colonial histories: the system may now be seen as open or permeable, but

115

it is possible to acknowledge external influences of various kinds without recognizing the depths of externally-generated internal transformation. The redefinition of anthropological interests, the development of an extended anthropological practice, the reconstitution of history, and the critique of evolution, are exercises which seem to operate at different levels, but which should be mutually implicated in an effort to transform this sort of intellectual practice.

9

The look of events

In some sense happenings are always at once outcomes, expressions and intrusions, but different frames of knowing render them unevenly across these terms. If history is seen as a 'concatenation of discrete and transitory entities or events, each unique in its particulars' (Ingold 1986: 74–5), events stand as outcomes of contingent causes in an immediate sense but have an unpredictable and somewhat arbitrary character when viewed from a distance. Things of great consequence may take place for trivial and adventitious reasons, as the nursery rhyme insists:

> For want of a nail
> The shoe was lost,
> For want of a shoe
> The horse was lost,
> For want of a horse
> The rider was lost,
> For want of a rider
> The battle was lost,
> For want of a battle
> The kingdom was lost,
> And all for the want
> Of a horse shoe nail.

Hence the profound distrust among historians of the more conventional, uncompromisingly empiricist, kind for any sort of deterministic model like the Marxian scheme. Even explanations of a much lower order encounter the suspicious attitude of pathological caution, the fearful circumspection so mindful of the plurality of causes and the multiplicity of aspects. Connections between a happening and some set of generative factors may be acknowledged, but these would not be charged with a systematic character, and would tend to be very much overshadowed by the force of the event itself. The master scheme of narrative is thus constituted through singular effect, rather than through process. Temporal flow might seem to have no structure, although readers of history encounter narrative tropes and forms again and again: careers develop, nations are built, empires decline.

In sociology or anthropology it is different. Codes of meaning or arrays of

117

behavioural rules are not immediately 'caused'. They are expressive in a circular way, or functional and mutually determining. If events are discussed at all, they lack the singular character of the historical deed or accident. In the notion of a speech act or in some other cultural enactment we find the event much reduced in relation to the generative scheme. What takes place has no life as an intrusion with a loose and partly unfixed causality, but is rather the expression of a structure, the manifestation of a cultural order or a set of notions about behaviour.

Hence the stereotypic form which events usually take in anthropological monographs which have as their essential objects the form or order of a system. We are told that when a father dies, the son must initiate certain ceremonies, and so on; this is the generalized and abstracted rendering of an event which may also be offered in an apparently more immediate guise – a specific case, with located and named persons. But the function of this specificity is generally validation rather than information – just as urban legends are authenticated through spurious detail. This is so because the names of people or their clans do not mean anything unless there is a serious account of lived context, of village histories, micropolitics, squabbles and biographies. This dimension of particularity and narrative is found in some better ethnographies, but is generally submerged because of the tension which arises with projects toward an order and coherence. Events or cases stripped of context thus carry only the weight of instances and exemplifications.

The difficulties that one might have in the abstract with this discourse are immeasurably sharpened by the fact that we speak of a colonized world, and one in which post-colonial states have not ceased to intervene in the lives of tribal and dependent populations within their borders. (Since the west acknowledges and celebrates the 'heated' character of its own history, there is no need to assert that here.) There is thus a gulf between theories of events or history which render change as the other side of the coin of stereotypic reproduction or enactment and the circumstances of the ethnographic world the discourse claims to be about. Fabian has pointed out that anthropology creates a false temporal distance between anthropological knowers and contemporary others who are in fact our coevals (1983). This removal of (paradigmatically) tribal Others to another time has, of course, larger ideological dimensions. A convergent political blindness arises from the exclusions I have concentrated upon: when lives are shot through by the savage changes and novel inequalities arising directly or indirectly from the conjunction of local and global dynamics, it seems something of an absurdity that anthropology should continue to privilege the anti-temporal field of relations, frame of meanings, or cultural logic which bestows positional values on the orderly march of people and their thoughts and doings.

Detective stories of the conventional puzzle kind occasion a different line of thought about events. The murder itself is initially a paradigmatically intrusive event: it comes as a shock to people and a threat to a regulated and comfortable bourgeois existence. Nothing could stand in a more problematic relation to categories and understandings. Except that, as the detective proceeds, it becomes apparent that the tidy community had a life at odds with its self-depiction: a forest of motives, resentments, and grounds for suspicion develops. This amounts not merely to the disclosure of context which makes the event explicable, but an overpowering super-contextualization which makes the act of murder a logical outcome of every suspect's grievances and opportunities. If one sets aside the fact that things are never the same again, the event collapses into the enactment of context, the consequence of relations and perceptions (and this is in fact the sort of solution offered in Bradd Shore's 'Samoan mystery' (1982) to a murder in the ethnographic field). This surfeit of motive, this permeating abundance of sense and causality, is the condition which anthropological discourse sets up. This not only drowns particulars, but defeats the attempt to delineate causes and reasons, since in their multiplicity they overlap and overdetermine. What the detective does is different, and entails diminishing much of the context, since one gathers, as the logic of the problem is exposed, that certain circumstances were less consequential than others, that points of apparent importance recede, that accusations lacked the grounding they appeared to possess at the time. Sometimes the heart of the matter lies in the distant past and sometimes elsewhere – in Conan Doyle it emerges from colonized places like India and, ironically, the Andaman Islands; events are thus traced to a deeper logic, whose longer-term dynamics are determinant rather than inescapably plural.

Conclusions

Renewed interest in the history of our discipline and disciplined inquiry into the history of confrontation between anthropology and its Other are therefore not escapes from empiry; they are practical and realistic. They are ways to meet the Other on the same ground, in the same Time.   Johannes Fabian, *Time and the other*

The central points of the arguments I have worked through can be distilled as follows. In an effort to present these as plainly as possible, I leave behind the many qualifications and footnotes of the preceding discussions.

1. It must be acknowledged that anthropoloy, like other specialist discourses, operates through practice like culture in general, and is therefore governed by something other than rationalist expectations. Practitioners of the discipline may aspire to be scientific, but models of how research *should* be conducted do not adequately describe it as it *is* conducted. Prescriptive epistemology, whether of a positivist or hermeneutic kind, therefore has very

little direct relevance for either the retrospective analysis of anthropological thought or the theoretical elaboration of appropriate methods for future research. Anthropology is a knowledge-producing practice which has taken place, and continues to take place, in institutional and (usually) colonial contexts. These are the contexts in which evidence is assembled; the factors which determine theoretical orientations and methods are the same as those which shape the form of evidence. There are no clear cut separations between theory, methods and evidence. Data has no fixity independent of evolving intellectual styles and quarrels. The assumptions of ethnographic descriptions may therefore be transmitted to theoretical works which innocently take sources to be unproblematic.

2. This epistemological stance helps one – or at least has helped me – to distinguish effective premises and hidden agendas from the stated rationales of anthropological texts. It permits a critique of the founding relations of anthropological discourse.

3. The omission of history from anthropological description and analysis is not some kind of contingent oversight but constitutes a systematic exclusion. The exclusion of historical processes was a necessary element in the professionalization of the discipline, and has been perpetuated because, at the most general level, the object of study has not changed. This object was and is essentially a social or cultural system or structure out of time. Explanations and interpretations have depended on the coherence of whichever elements of the system are privileged in a particular form of analysis, rather than upon processes entailing at once the positional or functional significance of systemic elements and their historic causality. The number of ethnographic studies which have actually broken from this orientation is small; substantially smaller than the number which claim some sort of historical orientation.

4. The ahistorical approach has led to at least two kinds of problems. First, the links between the routine functioning of a system, change, and historical transformations, have never been effectively theorized. This has been so because systems are relatively orderly while what lies outside them is, by definition, unsystematic. The focus upon the coherence or reproduction of 'culture' or 'society' out of time makes 'history' an unstructured, incoherent residue of contingent events.[1]

Second, there are many specific misinterpretations which treat particular social or cultural phenomena in terms of their positional, systemic value, when they manifestly derive from more or less recent historical change. Leaving aside the erroneous assumption that the indigenous culture has remained unchanged or developed autonomously for a long period, such interpretations are not always wrong, because of course events do acquire

120

social and cultural significance. However, the account must always be partial and misleading in so far as systematic logic is taken as a sufficient explanation.

5. (a) The exclusion of history and disciplinary professionalization have also resulted in the exclusion of the ethnographic writings of those other than professional anthropologists. The bases for this generalized exclusion are highly questionable. The quality of missionary descriptions, for instance, is very uneven, but the properties of the descriptive discourse and the familiarity with indigenous peoples upon which statements were typically based encourage one to place these texts, as a general category, on the same level as those of professionals. Judgements about the worth of particular texts can only be made on a case-by-case basis, and depend as much on the project of the reader as the intrinsic features of the text.

(b) Historical documents which are not ethnographic descriptions are often vitally important in an entirely different way. They provide the basis for a knowledge of the events which have had an impact upon the groups being studied; many tribal ethnographies have ignored these processes which other studies have shown to have had crucial ramifications for the system being considered. Texts which are thus worthless in ethnographic terms cannot be overlooked unless historical causality is denied. The theoretical obstacles and difficulties are confounded by practical factors, because most anthropologists lack historical training, are unaware of what kinds of sources exist, how they need to be pursued, and how they must be contextualized and evaluated. Taking a few rich sources out of context and using these as a quarry for ethnographic data does not amount to practising historical research.

6. A consequence of point 4 has been that various attempts to incorporate time or history into anthropology have been unsuccessful because the anthropological object has not been reformulated. Discussions such as Bourdieu's and Sahlins' can therefore deal with some time-scales, and with representations of history, but cannot effectively integrate real history. These attempts retain the central notion of system or structure but insist on its grounding in time. This grounding cannot effectively incorporate real history unless 'system' is displaced by 'systemic process' as the object of analysis.

7. The notion of history as a systemic process is circuitously derived from social evolutionary theory but breaks from it in several crucial ways. Notions of 'stages' and 'direction' are displaced by transformations which, in regional contexts, are not directional. The standard evolutionary logic of taking one contemporary society as the primitive form of another is totally fallacious. The substitute for what has been justly derided as conjectural history can be based upon ordinary historical analysis (where sources are available), archaeology, and sometimes other techniques such as linguistic

121

reconstruction. These methods always involve some speculation, and, in some cases, can only furnish a general and coarse-grained image. The question of their plausibility and value can only be established in particular regional contexts. It is manifest in the Pacific.

8. A consequence of point 5 (b) for the view of history as a systemic process is a breakdown of the division which has generally been sustained in anthropology between the coherence of traditional systems and the haphazard and disruptive course of subsequent history. Interpretations of the latter have generally been much weaker than those of the former. Satisfactory analysis would depend on treating, for example, metropolitan intrusions into tribal territory as a structured process like that of the indigenous system, and it would be unwise to pretend that such analysis would be easy. However, this is an especially important area for investigation, because it bears more directly upon contemporary tribal and third-world problems than many issues which are currently more central to anthropological discussion. This is not to say that some inquiries which are completely detached from this neo-colonial context are not worthwhile – since some bear indirectly on such problems anyway – but that it is inappropriate for the discipline to retain a focus which actually marginalizes such politically salient interests.

9. Many anthropological discussions which apparently have nothing in common with older forms of evolutionary discourse and are not even concerned with questions of social change retain evolutionary premises. These may occasionally be expressed in, for example, contrasts between types of societies but are often heavily obscured by apparently relativistic concepts and judgements. The criticism of such material can only be effected through an epistemology which takes apart the notions which animate particular texts; the more straightforward exercise which equates a stated position or assumptions with actual generative premises cannot get to the heart of the problem.

10. A refocussed anthropological vision would often take a greater interest in archaeological evidence about longer-term social change. It would also deal much more extensively with historical events and their consequences: this evidence would assume the same sort of importance that observed ethnographic minutiae and informants' statements now carry. Fieldwork would be decentred but not displaced: it is the conjunction of such intimate knowledge with short- and long-term history which has great potential in social and cultural analysis, not the pursuit of one endeavour to the exclusion of the other.

Afterword to the second edition (1996)

Since this book was written, the divide between history and anthropology has become increasingly fuzzy. There are many more strong works grounded in one discipline that draw upon the research methods and theoretical insights of the other. In anthropology, it is also notable that an antagonism between symbolic interpretation and historical contextualization that remained conspicuous in Melanesian studies up to the end of the 1980s has broken down: the richest work now links cosmology and ritual with apocalyptic local Christianities and local constructions of cash-cropping and mining (cf. Foster 1995: chapter 1).

If all books are difficult to write for different reasons, I found this one difficult because I felt a need to criticize notions that were at once widely discredited yet also seemed curiously alive. On the one hand, evolutionism seemed old-fashioned and distant from the point of view of much contemporary anthropology; on the other, evolutionary metaphors seemed still to inform much writing, especially when broad-brush comparisons were being made. This is still more the case today: a recent discussion of Melanesian political forms by a well-known figure in the field exhibits precisely the from–to logic that I questioned (Godelier 1992), while, at a much broader level, narratives of progression through successive social states have gained a new lease on life in the literature on postmodernism and post-colonialism.

Because I sought to draw attention to discredited but persistent features of anthropological rhetoric, *Out of time* unavoidably adopted a critical attitude toward recent scholarship and thus risked recapitulating one of the features of intellectual practice that it described. Writers of all kinds as well as scholars define the singularity and importance of their work not only by making positive claims but also by reifying and disparaging the work of predecessors. In the specifically academic context, this has often been effected through the formation of disciplines and new specialisms, and through moments of professionalization and reprofessionalization. Radcliffe-Brown's Australian monograph, discussed in chapter 2, exemplifies the tendency to negate the research of predecessors in order to create a new space for authoritative writing. Most pessimistically, historical anthropology might be seen as another such exercise in subdisciplinary invention.

Little would be gained, however, by the relativization of all scholarly projects. The Radcliffe-Brown case is egregious because the dismissal of predecessors was in no sense warranted by a substantial advance effected in Radcliffe-Brown's own ethnography. In other cases meaningful gains are made, and this is surely true of the one that this book sought to contextualize and consolidate: even if new competences in archival research are demanded of anthropologists, the aim was never to create a novel field with its criteria for admission and gatekeepers but rather to give all anthropological projects a measure of historical sophistication. But the point that knowledge proceeds through negation has a range of implications for the arguments of *Out of time*. In chapter 6, I was concerned to 'rescue' pre-professional anthropological writers such as missionaries and travellers, and this effort of affirmation may have suggested that I took the view that these colonial accounts were, in principle, just as good (or just as bad) as those of (professional) anthropologists. Certainly Johannes Fabian, in a generous review, felt the need to point out that missionaries' blindnesses and biases, and those of other travellers, could not be forgotten (1991: 60). I can only agree with the need to extend the provisional characterizations offered here, and I have drawn upon Fabian's work in my own subsequent analyses of evangelical discourse (e.g. 1992a).

The best restatement or reformulation of my point might be that *all* observations and narratives concerning other peoples need to be scrutinized. While it may very frequently be the case that anthropological descriptions are more insightful and less prejudiced than those of antecedents, the professional discipline is too general and crude a factor to itself determine the character or quality of particular texts. The interpretation of anthropological history in a sequence beginning with amateurs and leading through phases of professionalization could indeed be seen as another evolutionary narrative of the kind this book sought to make more explicit.

Of course, the suggestion that we (anthropologists) needed to engage more rigorously and expansively with a range of earlier sources concerning the societies studied was grounded in other arguments too. Most importantly, the point was not that these accounts were necessarily 'good' or 'bad', sufficient or insufficient, in themselves but that they contained vital information concerning earlier social and cultural forms, and the historical constitution of the phenomena witnessed ethnographically, that were simply unobtainable in other ways. In the case of the Pacific, mariners', colonists' and missionaries' texts can be and need to be read against the grain, in the fashion that has perhaps been most explicitly engaged in by Bronwen Douglas (e.g. 1995). (How it is adequately done is, moreover, explored and exemplified at some length in Sahlins' most recent publication [1995]).

As Pels and Salemink (n.d.) have recently pointed out, anticolonialism in anthropology enabled another phase of professionalization, the creation of a higher kind of scholarship that disavowed the contamination of engagement in policy. The professionalizing effort is witnessed again, not only in that more recent phase of the discipline's history and also in this book's own construction of a historical anthropology, but most conspicuously in the formation of the new discipline of cultural studies, which presumes the contamination of anthropology by colonial engagement and abrogates to itself the capacity to engage critically with the object of culture. Given that the problematic aspects of the project are being discussed as much within the field as without (e.g. Frow 1995), these debates need not be reviewed here; though, given the perspective of this book, it is appropriate to note that cultural studies cannot represent an advance on anthropology while it remains obsessively focussed on contemporary texts, and while its interest in historical contextualization is negligible.

Out of time bracketed off the question of the distinctiveness of indigenous constructions of time and history. It did so strategically, in order to focus upon other sets of issues that were in part concerned with the constitution of anthropological knowledge and in part with ways of accounting for longer-term social transformations, in Oceania in particular. My interest in the latter set of questions stemmed from a background in archaeology; though I remain of the view that theorising those longer-term dynamics should continue to be a significant area of mutual concern for anthropology and archaeology, the issues patently lack contemporaneity and urgency from the point of view of most anthropologists today.

In a critique of this book, David Hanlon (1992: 118–19) noted very fairly that the question of E. H. Carr's classic, *What is history?* (1961) was never addressed in a concerted way. Moreover, Bradd Shore complained that, while anthropologists were berated on various counts in *Out of time,* 'History' was taken as an unproblematic category (1992: 123). I am far more sympathetic to the first response than the second. Shore's review made it plain that he had not read the book closely, or at least had not understood it (for a detailed response see Thomas 1992b). It was quite clear that I was not advocating the encompassment of anthropological interpretation by something like conventional empirical narrative history but was interested instead, on the one hand, in an account of social transformations shorn of all the teleologies and temporal metaphors of evolutionism and, on the other, in a refinement of Sahlins' structural history that accommodated the interenactment of colonial structures as well as the transformation of structure that he so consummately identified. While my arguments here were for the most part polemical and programmatic, I did attempt to demonstrate how these theoretical perspectives might actually be realized through case studies in a subsequent book, *Entangled objects* (Thomas 1991).

As Hanlon had pointed out, however, this was not to do justice to the modalities of indigenous temporal and historical understanding. The book would have been richer, in particular, had I engaged with Polynesian ideas of political transformation, which can and have been explored via myth (e.g. Sissons 1989); or

125

had I been able to take into account Marilyn Strathern's arguments concerning 'first contacts' in Melanesia. Strathern (1990) argued essentially that the arrival of whites in New Guinea was more like the appearance of an image in a ceremonial context than an 'event' as we ('Westerners') understand it. Although an argument specifically from Melanesian modes of perception, this would destabilize both Sahlins' argument concerning Cook and my own, to the extent that the capacity of these contacts to figure as 'events' that have consequences for the order of indigenous culture is denied. Strathern's tantalisingly brief comments do not, of course, amount to an extended account of Melanesian historical (or unhistorical) imaginings, though I note that Ballard (1992) has put forward a fuller argument along similar lines for Huli.

It would not be good enough, though, if these explorations of indigenous notions and perceptions simply produced a set of discrete ethnographic accounts. In that case, anthropological relativism would merely have been extended into another area: where we already had a proliferation of other cultures, socialities and sexualities, we would now have many historicities. Acknowledging cultural difference and plurality is important as a moment of research and understanding but inadequate as a conclusion. The peoples that bear these differing historicities and cultures are, we need to remember, not a set of mutually isolated groups. We would not know them as anthropological cases if their lives had not been connected with our own, at whatever remove.

To connect the 'cultures' anthropologists study and the formation of knowledge via colonial relationships is not to presume that either the cultures or the knowledge are pervasively structured by the larger historical dynamic of colonialism. It is not to presume that local perceptions and cultural differences have been effaced and homogenized by a global process, or that local meanings have necessarily been defined by colonial relationships. In some cases, they have been, but it may also be true, elsewhere, that even oppressive colonial forces do not transform or hegemonize local historical understandings and narratives. But where this is so, it attests to singular historical effect rather than the lack of historical effect. While the tension and interplay of colonial and local histories need to be explored in particular cases, this is why, in principle, an anthropological history must engage both with the history of anthropological knowledge and with the dynamics of the local.

References to afterword

Ballard, Chris (1992) First contact as a non-event in the New Guinea highlands. Paper presented at the American Anthropological Society meetings, San Francisco, December 1992

Carr, E. H. (1961) *What is history?* London: Macmillan

Douglas, Bronwen (1995) Power, discourse, and the appropriation of God: Christianity and subversion in a Melanesian context. *History and Anthropology* **9**: 57–92

Fabian, Johannes (1991) Anthropology against time. *Transition* **1** (3): 55–61

Foster, Robert J. (1995) *Social reproduction and history in Melanesia.* Cambridge: Cambridge University Press

Frow, John (1995) *Cultural studies and cultural value.* Oxford: Oxford University Press

Godelier, Maurice (1992) An unfinished attempt at reconstructing the social processes which may have prompted the transformation of great-men societies into big-men societies. In Maurice Godelier and Marilyn Strathern (eds.), *Big men and great men: personifications of power in Melanesia.* Cambridge: Cambridge University Press

Hanlon, David (1992) Time is history? [Book review forum]. *Pacific Studies* **15**: 118–22

Pels, Peter and Oscar Salemink (n.d.) Introduction: the colonial subjects of anthropology. MS

Sahlins, Marshall (1995) *How 'natives' think, about Captain Cook, for example.* Chicago: University of Chicago Press

Shore, Bradd (1992) *Out of tune* [Book review forum]. *Pacific Studies* **15**: 122–35

Sissons, Jeffrey (1989) The seasonality of power: the Rarotongan legend of Tangiia. *Journal of the Polynesian Society* **98**: 331–47

Strathern, Marilyn (1990) Artefacts of history: events and the interpretation of images. In Jukka Siikala (ed.), *Culture and history in the Pacific.* Helsinki: Transactions of the Finnish Anthropological Society

Thomas, Nicholas (1991) *Entangled objects: exchange, material culture and colonialism in the Pacific.* Cambridge, Mass.: Harvard University Press

(1992a) Colonial conversions: difference, hierarchy, and history in early twentieth century evangelical propaganda. *Comparative Studies in Society and History* **34** (2): 366–89

(1992b) Historical anthropology and the politics of critique. *Pacific Studies* **15**: 142–58

Notes

Introduction

1. I can also save confusion in a minor instance by indicating that I use the term 'colonial history' broadly, to mean histories of any kind of intrusion by metropolitan powers in less developed territories, rather than in the much narrower sense of periods of formal colonial rule; the use of the stricter meaning in some conservative history often implies that there is no informal domination in the absence of overt administration.
2. The Lévi-Strauss essay was first published in 1949. See Kuper (1973: 162–4) for a brief discussion of the significance of the Evans-Pritchard article.

1 History and anthropological discourse

1. It is notable that reviews of works of history or historical anthropology very frequently raise questions about the adequacy of non-anthropological source materials (such as missionaries' writings), making invidious comparisons between these and ethnographic observations (e.g. Bloch 1987). It is as though this is a general weakness which can simply be pointed out: there is no need to demonstrate that the faults of these sources actually introduce errors in description or analysis. In most anthropological accounts there are, however, invariably comparable sources of 'bias', such as the preponderance of senior men amongst informants, but this has only been discussed extensively in the context of feminist critique, and is certainly a rare point for comment in book reviews.
2. Evans-Pritchard's essays on the topic (1962) made a number of points with which I can only agree, but these could hardly be seen to have borne fruit in the British context. A collection of history and anthropology was published by the Association of Social Anthropologists (Lewis (ed.) 1968) on the basis of their 1966 conference; the institutional origins of the volume enable one to regard it as reasonably representative of thought at the time. What is notable about the essays, however, is that there are really none which go far toward *integrating* historical and anthropological methods or concerns. Those by historians simply show that some anthropological concepts are of interest in the interpretation of past societies, and some of those by anthropologists lean toward conventional history (e.g. Ardener) whilst others set up a kind of interaction while reinforcing the division between objects of study (Morton-Williams). One concerned with Albania aims partly to establish 'a picture of the traditional social structure of the country' (Whittaker 1968: 253), which is as unhistorical a notion as one is likely to encounter.

3. Even a recent, sophisticated collection on foragers is ambiguous on this matter: 'Foraging peoples have played an important role in human history. They represent the original condition of humankind, the system of production that prevailed during virtually 99 per cent of human history. Having said that, it is important to make two caveats. First, contemporary or recent foragers are not living fossils, their history and their distance from humanity's ancestors are as long as those of all human groups. It is their economy and technology that make foragers so important for science. They represent a basic human adaptation without the accretions and complications brought about by agriculture, cities, states, advanced technology, and national and class conflict. Second, foraging people are not isolates, they are living in the twentieth century and are moulded in part by that context' (Leacock and Lee 1982: 5).

The question here is whether the recognition of the latter factors overrides the basic presumptions expressed in the first two sentences. A point which is only mentioned later (*ibid*: 13), which qualifies those propositions much more heavily than the 'caveats', is that virtually all hunter-gatherer populations in Africa and Asia, as well as many of those elsewhere, have lived for thousands of years in direct and indirect contact, and frequently in competition, with those practising different modes of production. Although a number of writers have linked the features of some of these societies to the fact of their 'encapsulation', the necessary conclusion that such groups can be in no way representative of earlier foragers might be made more forcefully.

4. Leenhardt's ethnography (notably 1947) and some other anthropological works were incorporated into a manifesto of 'the Melanesian way' by the FLNKS (Kanak Socialist National Liberation Front) in New Caledonia or, as they prefer, Kanaké (Tjibaou and Missotte 1978).

2 Radcliffe-Brown, Geertz and the foundations of modern anthropology

1. Fortes maintained in 1949 that 'No living scholar has had so decisive an influence on the development of social anthropology' (1949a: ix; for his more extended considerations see Fortes 1969). This judgement would never have been shared by American anthropologists, who saw themselves as 'cultural' rather than 'social', but the fact that Radcliffe-Brown's work had some impact on the discipline in the United States is reflected in the number of American contributions to the volume of essays edited by Fortes in honour of his work (five out of eleven). In this brief section I do not attempt a full review of Radcliffe-Brown's work, or even of his earlier work. For fuller discussion see Kuper 1973; chapter 2; Evans-Pritchard 1981: 200–2; Langham 1981; and, for the most extended and historically balanced treatment, Stocking 1984.

2. Leach, for instance, described him as a 'fraud' (1977: 6).

3. This is still the dominant view, but, as I argue below (chapter 6), many missionaries and others did in fact combine an ethnographic vision with extended personal inquiry.

4. Langham (1981: 245). Langham's analysis has been criticized on some important points (Stocking 1984: 135n; Urry 1983), but this particular argument has not been challenged.

5. This question is significant from the point of view of contemporary theory, because the development of archaeological techniques (and secure dating in particular) since the time of Radcliffe-Brown's formulations now make it possible to know about some past events and processes. It is another question as to

whether this kind of knowledge can be readily integrated with the anthropological knowledge of modern or recent societies. It is also the case that Radcliffe-Brown's prescription assumes that all groups studied by anthropologists are like the Andamanese in the sense that there is no literary documentation of events prior to European contact, but many of the societies studied by anthropologists (e.g. in Asia) possessed bodies of textual material and inscriptions, or were mentioned in texts produced by others. (The question of the status of indigenous oral traditions and their value for historical reconstruction is a vexed one.) Of course, literary materials such as epics and genealogical narratives might be dismissed because they often do not deal with what westerners recognize as 'history', but that difficulty should perhaps prompt questions about our category, rather than the rejection of such source materials.

A further point of some consequence in this context is the persistence of the conflation of history and speculative schema of one sort or another. In Augé's recent essay on 'Symbol, function [and] history' in anthropological thought, the third term is roughly equated with 'evolution' or 'evolution/diffusion' (1982: 10–16). There is no reference to eventful, socially immediate history.

6. A rare indication of the extent of some of the effects of contact emerges from a footnote of Radcliffe-Brown's acknowledging his difficulty in obtaining information concerning sexual notions: 'the natives of the Great Andaman at the present time show an unusual prudery in their conversation and dealings with white men, but there is good reason to suspect that this is due to the influence of officers who have been in charge of the Andaman home [a welfare and surveillance institution] in recent years' (1922: 321–2n).

7. That R. H. Mathews' work was unjustly criticized was established by Elkin (1956: 249–50; see also Langham 1981: 290–1). It is somewhat ironic that Radcliffe-Brown should raise questions about other investigators' informants, since some of his own research was with Aborigines transported from their tribal areas to hospitals for those suffering from venereal disease; much of the material was derived from 'communities decimated by contact with white society' (Langham 1981: 265). The significance of the Australian monograph is apparent from a statement of Fortes: 'in my personal perspective … the modern era in the study of kinship and social organization is first firmly established with the publication of Radcliffe-Brown's 1931 monograph' (1969: 42). It must be pointed out, however, that Fortes' especially high regard for Radcliffe-Brown's work lies at one end of a spectrum. There has also been a long-running debate about allegations that he plagiarized the work of his sometime collaborator, Daisy Bates (Needham 1974; White 1981).

8. My point here is not that Radcliffe-Brown had some sort of conscious master-plan for displacing those unfortunate enough to attempt serious ethnography before its time, but that this was the effect of practices and statements such as those expressed in this text. This situation arose from a conjunction of scientist attitudes and the process of professionalization, and the personal empathies or antipathies of writers such as Radcliffe-Brown to their predecessors are not especially important. As the more detailed studies of Langham, Stocking and others make plain, the transition to a professional discipline was far more fuzzy than anthropologists later generally perceived, but the complex interactions between teachers, disciples, rivals, institutions, etc., are beyond my vision here.

9. It should be emphasized that this section is not a discussion of the totality of Geertz's work, but is simply concerned to establish the very basic features which the 'interpretive anthropology' approach shares with the perspective of Radcliffe-

Brown. A substantial component of Geertz's work (such as that on Indonesian agricultural change) is not to be subsumed under the 'interpretive anthropology' label, and I do not expect that he would, in any case, put forward the same formulations today. However, his most influential texts have expressed the 'interpretive' position. For further discussion of his work see Marcus and Fischer (1986: *passim*) and, for a more critical view, Austin (1979); see also the responses to her essay by Wagner, Sharrock, Barnes and others, which appear in the same issue of *Social Analysis*.

I would add, though, that while Geertz's later book, *Negara* (1980), might appear to be a work of historical anthropology, this is true only in the very limited sense that it draws on historical sources concerning nineteenth-century Balinese polities. The orientation is in fact toward abstracting the elements of an ideal type (the theatre state) and showing that this persisted in different historical contexts, as is apparent in many passages such as 'the expressive nature of the Balinese state was apparent through the whole of its known history' (1980: 13); the 'divine king cult' is attributed with an 'essentially constant cultural form' (*ibid*: 125), and so on. The book deals avowedly with a synchronic entity rather than one which has social or historical dynamics.

10 This emphasis is partly justified on the basis of a tenet that if one wants to understand a science, attention should be paid not to theories or conclusions, but to 'what the practitioners of it do' (1973: 5). This is fine, but Geertz proceeded to ignore the fact that a typical anthropological career might consist of a few years' fieldwork and about thirty or forty years' writing and teaching – as well, perhaps, as such activities as acting as an advisor for ethnographic films or museum exhibitions, involvement in 'development' policy or implementation, making occasional public statements about current affairs in areas supposedly covered by one's expert knowledge, legal representations on behalf of indigenous peoples, and so on. What anthropologists do cannot be reduced to ethnography. I stress particularly that the practice of reading and interpreting anthropological literature in general – whether for teaching, or synthesizing, comparative purposes, or idle pleasure – is a necessary and not a contingent feature of anthropological practice. The questions of how information is derived from anthropological texts and subsequently used therefore has a bearing on the discipline's epistemology, and this is why I discuss in chapters 4 and 5 the effects of Handy's Marquesan ethnography – and museum research in general – in Goldman's analytic synthesis of the Polynesian material.

11. This formulation makes anthropologists' research on their own societies radically marginal to the concept of the discipline; the existence of such research is acknowledged, significantly, only in a footnote (1973: 14n).

3 The background to Polynesian anthropology

1. For an overview of European perceptions of the Pacific in the eighteenth and nineteenth centuries, see Smith's justly celebrated *European vision and the South Pacific* (1960); for a rather orthodox review of Pacific history (there being no other) see Howe (1984); and, for the later development of anthropological and particularly archaeological research, see Kirch (1984: 1–13). Forster is discussed by Hoare (1976).

2. The other main exception is Hogbin's work on Ontong Java (e.g. 1931).

3. A recent collection (Stocking 1985) deals with anthropology in museums, but not particularly with museum-sponsored ethnographic research projects, or the form of ethnographic discourse generated by such work.

4 An evolutionary argument and its sources

1. Goldman's book is also celebrated and drawn upon extensively by Sherry Ortner in her appraisal of Polynesian gender relations (1981), which appeared in an influential collection of symbolic studies of gender and sexuality. I have elsewhere argued (1986b) that misinterpretations in her analysis derive substantially from an over-reliance upon Goldman.

   It is obviously not the point of the present discussion to assess the empirical adequacy of Goldman's book in great detail. But since the general view is charitable, it should be stressed that Goldman's lack of personal research experience in the Pacific and dependence on mainly inadequate secondary materials lead to many minor errors. A typical mistake which no-one more familiar with the Pacific would make is his use of the missionary Gunn's reminiscences (1914) in the section on Futuna (1970: 334), obviously without realizing that Gunn's Futuna was a completely different island, part of what is now Vanuatu in the western Pacific, and not the place north-east of Fiji which forms part of the modern French territory of Wallis and Futuna. Cambridge, Massachusetts, is not Cambridge, England. By any standard this is simply carelessness, but it should be pointed out that my criticism of Goldman's work in general draws on historical knowledge and a perspective which was not available at the time he wrote the book; he says that it was essentially complete in 1966 (1970: xiii), which was the year in which the *Journal of Pacific History* was launched, and about the time when accessible and detailed information about contact histories and the impact of colonialism began to appear. Since then, knowledge of early Polynesian societies and of the kinds of documentation available has increased very considerably. I cannot therefore criticize his analysis for failing to incorporate material which was scarcely available at the time, but I do believe that even consideration of standard reactions to evolutionism, and the sorts of question raised by Evans-Pritchard's 'History and anthropology' essay (1962) might have motivated some conceptual reworking.

2. Goldman starts with the New Zealand Maori who exemplify the traditional system. Manihiki and Rakahanga (considered conjointly) and Tongareva (all in the Cook Islands), which follow, are not seen as later developments but as 'examples of Maori structure as adapted to the smaller conditions of atolls' (1970: 27). Easter Island, the Marquesas and Mangaia (in the Cook Islands) are variants of the open type; again, the order of presentation is not supposed to reflect any developmental rank. However, Mangareva, the Societies, and Hawaii, 'the three Stratified societies of eastern Polynesia suggest an approximate evolutionary sequence' (1970: 27). In western Polynesia, Samoan societies are open while Tonga 'equates with Tahiti and Hawaii as a Stratified society' (1970: 24). The other western Polynesian groups are considered as variants on 'the Samoa–Tonga type' and are not ranked 'in any evolutionary order' (1970: 27–8). There is thus a clear difference of method in the presentation of eastern and western material; I shall argue later that this is of some theoretical consequence.

   The choice of New Zealand as a starting point is curious because it is likely to have been the *last* place in Polynesia to be settled (Kirch 1984: 74–9), and therefore its social forms would surely be expected to reflect late and distinctive developments (especially since the two large islands contrast geographically and ecologically with the rest of Polynesia in every significant respect). There can be no prior justification for seeing the three Cook Islands cases as adaptations *of* this pattern; if one group of societies must be seen as a locally adapted form of

133

the other – and this is not the only possible explanatory strategy – it would be more plausible to see the more recently settled, peripheral case as logically subordinate to the central area.

3. In the analysis itself, Goldman moves between partial repudiation of this type of logic, and its thinly veiled employment. Thus in the chapter on the Marquesas, he writes

> The divergence from Maori is solely in pattern of organization arising from specific emphases on different issues. Thus even if we have no assurance that the Marquesan Open was an actual historical development from a specifically Maori Traditional there is good reason to regard the Marquesan system as a structural variant of a type similar to that of Maori. (1970: 133)

At a more particular level, many distinctive features of the systems in the Marquesas and Manihiki/Rakahanga (for example) are discussed in terms of similarity with or variation upon Maori forms (1970: 58–64 *passim*; 132, 146, 148).

4. The chapter of Lewis's to which I refer was originally published in *Man* in 1966.
5. Out of the eighteen 'societies' studied, the accounts of eleven are exclusively or nearly exclusively based on Bishop Museum publications (which had a standard form and which were mainly based on the research of museum staff). In five more cases, Bishop Museum documentation, or other work by Peter Buck or E. S. C. Handy of the Museum, was significant. Buck's approach must be seen as particularly important, since his writing is a major source, if not the only source, for no fewer than five of the societies. Ian Hogbin's papers and Firth's much more extensive works provided the basis for Goldman's discussions of the outliers of Ontong Java and Tikopia respectively. In these two cases alone, the sources reflected the British structural-functionalist tradition rather than a primarily American, trenchantly empiricist, pre-functionalist museum anthropology.

It is not surprising that the Polynesian groups not considered by Goldman were precisely those for which there was no Bishop Museum publications. Despite the fact that Rarotonga sustained the largest population in the Cook Islands, and became the dominant place within the group, it is not discussed, although Rarotongan culture is well documented through the missionary Gill's publications (e.g. 1876a, b, 1916), among many others (see Gilson 1980). Tuvalu (formerly the Ellice Islands) was the only group never visited by a Bishop Museum expedition; ethnographic bulletins on Rapa and Rurutu in the Austral Islands were prepared (Stokes n.d.; Seabrook n.d.) but never published. Although research was conducted in the Tuamotus, and archaeological reports and translations of myths were issued, a general ethnography was never produced (cf. Buck 1945: 85). Thus Tuvalu, the Australs and the Tuamotus do not figure in Goldman's analysis. It might also be noted that the extent to which Goldman deals with variation within groups reflects the pattern of Bishop Museum documentation. The Society Islands are treated as a monocultural entity, as they were in Museum publications. For adventitious reasons, the Cooks were never visited by a large expedition but were rather dealt with by Buck in the course of several short trips, which resulted in separate bulletins on different islands. Thus Tongareva and Manihiki/Rakahanga in the northern Cooks are treated separately, while the much larger islands of Raiatea, Taha'a and Huahine are lumped together with Tahiti as part of the Society group. However, as Gunson has noted, evidence for social variation is 'too marked to be ignored' (1982: 68).

Sahlins' 1958 work similarly relied very heavily on the Bishop Museum bulletins, and paid no attention to areas (other than Tikopia and Ontong Java) which were not 'covered' by ethnographic bulletins. Essentially the same misinterpretations as I proceed to identify in Goldman's book are found in Sahlins' work, and in some cases these are exacerbated by the use of even more unreliable sources, such as Linton's (1939) subsequent synthesis of the Marquesan data, which is riddled with both minor and highly consequential empirical errors, overstatements, misinterpretations, etc. (see Dening 1980; Thomas 1989).

For further discussion of the context and premises of Bishop Museum research, see Borofsky's discussion (1987: 45–50) of the Pukapukan work of E. and P. Beaglehole (1938).

6. The initiation of this bold pan-Polynesian project had much to do with Herbert Gregory, a vigorous and enterprising Yale geologist who became Acting Director of the Museum in 1919 and was subsequently Director until 1936, when Peter Buck (who usually referred to himself by his Maori name, Te Rangi Hiroa) took over. Gregory actively developed the affiliation with Yale, which funded various fellowships, and was also apparently instrumental in securing philanthropic funding on a large scale for various expeditions. The first Pacific Science Congress was held in Hawaii in 1920 and seems to have fuelled the Bishop Museum's ethnographic venture. 'An outline of the scope and methods to be applied to Polynesia was formulated' and research was to take place 'under the headings of material culture and art, mythology and religion, social organization, language, music, and historical research' (Buck 1945: 44). A guide for fieldworkers along the lines of the British *Notes and Queries in Anthropology* was produced.

7. This notion is hardly a thing of the past: 'My focus will be the small island of Santa Catalina ... where the precolonial culture was best preserved' (Davenport 1986: 95) – an arbitrarily selected example.

8. As I shall argue below, the Bishop Museum writers frequently denigrated missionaries in general but did draw on missionary writings – although in an inconsistent and careless way (cf. next chapter). A curious feature of the pattern of their use of such sources was that any documents actually encountered in the island group where work was being carried out were worked over and often incorporated into the publication (usually only with partial acknowledgement), but there was never any effort made to track down relevant manuscripts by missionaries or anybody else elsewhere. Manuscripts concerning the Marquesas, Tahiti and various other groups which were actually in mission archives in Honolulu near the Museum were never examined, and of course there were no special trips to libraries in the mainland United States or Europe. Ethnography was the method of research, even though much of the information collected in the field was derived not from observation but from recollections or written materials.

9. This attitude is underlined by a comment of E. S. C. Handy on Williamson's *Social and political systems of central Polynesia* (1924), an extensive work based upon library research. Handy regrets that Williamson was unaware of the Bishop Museum research in the area (which in fact only began in 1920) and asserted that the 'full and authentic information' derived therefrom 'automatically relegated the literary sources to a position of secondary importance, and made unnecessary the laborious process of examination and deduction with which [Williamson] has filled three volumes' (Handy 1930: 4 n2).

The claim that library work is essentially redundant would have some plausibility if modern ethnographic research had in fact produced an intricate and satisfying picture of the 'traditional' cultures. This was certainly so in a few instances: it would have to be acknowledged that observations on Dumont D'Urville's 1820s voyage add little to Firth's incomparably rich account of Tikopian society. But the picture is different if not inverted for many of the islands and groups covered by Bishop Museum research. For some places like Tahiti an enormous range of early descriptions exist, while the complexities of colonial history and the mission presence make the results of fieldwork in the twenties or thirties both slim and problematic: Handy's text on the Society Islands was one of the sparsest of the Museum's publications. Although the view that salvage ethnography displaced literary sources is therefore untenable in its own terms, the key premise must be questioned: as I argue at greater length below, the whole style of comparison must be thrown out unless one supposes that knowledges of a place in 1820 and 1940 or 1980 are the same to the extent that they can be substituted for one another. It is as though a poor account from some period may be rejected, and a later description relied upon exclusively.

10. A correlate of this prior familiarity with culturally associated groups would, however, have been that knowledge of other places – and no doubt a developed sense of 'what Polynesia was like' – helped fill in the picture, biasing it towards a Polynesian or regional Polynesian type. Society Islands material might have overinfluenced that depiction of Mangareva, Tupuai and the Tuamotus, for instance. Goldman himself suspected that this took place in Buck's description of Tongareva, which he suggested 'portrays the traditional forms more strongly perhaps than they really were' (1970: 70).

11. This may seem a crude and overdrawn parallel, but the most cursory examination of publications on Tonga reveals that the influence of the elite there and that of the former Queen Salote in particular upon scholarship has been so considerable that many works have virtually had the character of official publications (e.g. Rutherford 1977). The problem in Polynesian studies of the circumscription of scholarship by chiefly perspectives has certainly not been restricted to the work of the Bishop Museum.

5 Untying evidence, rethinking transformations

1. The Marquesas are a group of six islands some 1,200 kilometres north-east of Tahiti. Before the period of early contact (roughly 1790–1820) the population was about 35,000, but fell very rapidly because of disease, and from the 1880s on was around 5,000 or less. Traditional subsistence was primarily agriculture (taro, yams, and especially breadfruit) and fishing. Topographically there were and are distinct separations between valleys, and the inhabitants – between a few hundred and about a thousand in number – constituted the main social groups. By the time of Handy's research the catastrophic depopulation, and the effects of the Catholic mission and French administration, had had very marked effects, although the involvement of the people in production for cash and wider markets was very limited until much later.

   The critique here is based on some much more extended studies. Rather than clutter the text with frequent citations, I simply refer the reader interested in further detail or documentation to my main work on the islands (Thomas 1990).

2. The basis of the account was strengthened by Handy's use of certain earlier exercises in salvage ethnography – the papers of Pierre Chaulet and Réné Dordillon in the archives of the Catholic mission at Taiohae. These, and particularly Chaulet's extensive manuscript essays, describe a wide range of

customs, rites and beliefs, and include legendary material and many specific listings of such things as the deities associated with particular activities or places. Chaulet arrived in the Marquesas in 1852 and, judging from his letters, took an interest in ethnography from the start. His informants were mainly indigenous priests (*tuhuna oʻono* and *tauʻa*) from Nukuhiva, but Chaulet also obtained material from informants from other parts of the group; he sometimes indicates that a rite (for example) was peculiar to an island or locality. Although Handy quotes or alludes to many passages, it is clear that his debt to these manuscripts goes beyond these particular references. Although many of the lesser mission sources were ignored, and the better ones were used in an erratic and undisciplined way, the account nonetheless benefited considerably from an extensive process of linguistically-sensitive observation and inquiry which took place between seventy and forty years before Handy's own research.

3. These labels carry an ideological burden, even though they may be used loosely. For discussion of Sahlins' more influential parallel between Polynesian chiefs and feudal lords, on one side, and Melanesian big-men and capitalist entrepreneurs, see Jolly (1987).

4. The outward manifestations of deference and respect might have been detected if observers had looked to these more particular contexts: 'Every chief seems to have considerable power *over his own dependants* in a certain way' (Darling, 1834–35: 10 April 1835; emphasis added). That there was some definite degree of control is also reflected in the capacities of particular chiefs such as Keoenui (on the island of Tahuata in the 1830s) to keep people away from missionaries' services if alienated from or offended by the mission in some way.

5. It might be noted here that a widespread strategy in contemporary anthropological debate involves identifying a particular feature of an earlier view as 'ethnocentric' and revising the interpretation along different theoretical lines. This is dishonest to the extent that it uses the unquestionable need to 'minimize bias' as a cover for theoretical difference. The fact that some sort of 'ethnocentrism' is a necessary and inevitable feature of any sort of discourse at all is ignored; some aspects of one's culture are obviously going to pass unscrutinized while others are contraposed to the other culture and used to animate an argument. The charge of ethnocentrism is thus always an argument about what should be discussed, rather than a serious critique of the properties of analysis.

6. The Catholic mission sometimes organised 'elections' at which mission-sponsored candidates were unanimously supported (Acar, Journal: 25 August 1895). Thomas Lawson, an English resident on 'Ua Huka who was engaged mainly in provisioning ships, attempted to see one man, Teikimoetina, declared the paramount chief of the island, so as to maintain a state of law and order (Lawson to Gulick, January 1868). Robert Louis Stevenson, who visited the Marquesas in 1888, met a man who was *kikino* (of servile status) but apparently chief of Taipi valley nevertheless (1900: 44–6).

7. Marquesans did distinguish between the epochs of indigenous people and 'the time of foreigners' (*te tai haoʻe*). There were probably more specific categories related to phases in the nineteenth century, but these are not documented, and are unlikely in any case to have corresponded with the ethnologist's desire to distinguish what was genuinely pre-contact. By the 1920s, the pre-contact period was really very remote, especially given the changes which had taken place, and the fact particularly that most priests, who were the traditional repositories of traditions and specialized knowledge, had died rather earlier.

8. A degree of idealization may be the source of discrepancies between Handy's

account of chieftainship and land relations, and the picture which can be derived from a reading of early sources. He stressed the likeness between the tribe and a family, and argued that the chief was a benevolent father figure who owned the land, just as a household head controls the family's resources (1923: 35, 42, 43, 53, 57–8). He noted that although the overall pattern 'was more or less communistic', there seemed in some parts of the group to be a 'feudal' tendency, 'under which the chief allotted sections of land to individual families and received in return a part of the produce and service in war or industry' (*ibid*: 57).

9. Edward Robarts wrote, for instance, that 'No chieftain can force a tribute from anyone excepting those on his own private estate' ([1974]: 266). Much later the missionary Chaulet similarly insisted that there was no sort of general chiefly ownership:

> I have sometimes heard from foreigners who talk about the Marquesas without knowing the customs that the chief is the master of his valley, and that he can dispose of it as he wishes. This is an error; I have always heard the natives say the opposite; I've always seen the opposite, which is simply natural and consistent with justice which says that you can't give what doesn't belong to you; certainly a chief who acted otherwise would formerly have caused a war. (Chaulet, AMS: 48–9)

Since statements to the contrary are made, this matter would seem hopelessly confused – unless one consults the evidence about what was actually done with land by various chiefly and non-chiefly people in the early years of contact and documentation. This is not the place to go into great detail about what can be derived from the missionary account and from Robarts' narrative, but it is apparent that certain chiefly men and women possessed considerable areas, but also that a number of people who were not of chiefly status had considerable holdings; some controlled canoes and fishing grounds as well as land. In some instances it is clear that these '*akatia* or 'persons of property' held land which they personally had expropriated from others.

It might be pointed out here that in Sahlins' evolutionary book (1958) the use of unreliable Bishop Museum sources permitted him to link distinct cases such as Marquesan society – where chiefs did not play a central role in redistributing surplus produce – with his overall stereotype of the chiefdom as a redistributive system. A closer analysis of detailed early accounts of Polynesian societies makes it clear that many societies in which chiefs were influential were not 'chiefdoms' in this sense.

10. This refers to the crucial item of regalia: girdles were to sovereignty as rings are to engagement.

11. The 'devolved' character of Rapanui society is virtually recognized in Goldman's earlier article (1955), but is suppressed or very much understated in the book because of its incompatibility with the overall argument.

12. The profound character of the movement away from chieftainship is also manifest in the distinct contexts of human sacrifice in the various islands. The practice of sacrifice in general arises from a need to deal with or incorporate some form of divine power. A specific sacrifice creates completeness in a relation between people and a god where there was previously a lack – produced either by some fault or transgression, or simply by the incompleteness of propitiation, which must be periodically repeated. Many activities such as fishing must be preceded by some minor sacrifice, which was carried out by the practitioner or on their behalf. The control of such minor and everyday sacrifices is not generally a matter of great political consequence, since their ends are often those of one person or a small group. Human sacrifice, on the other hand, is only connected

138

with matters of the most fundamental and general importance, which reflect the conditions of existence of society as a whole. In a system encompassed by kingship, the rulers' life crises are occasions for human sacrifice since, as Valeri points out, the existence of society is linked to the life of the royal personage: 'in these rites society is not distinguished from the person of the king who symbolizes it' (1985: 49–50). In Tahiti the main occasions for human victims seem to have been the birth and accession of paramount chiefs or *ari'i rahi*, when all the district chiefs brought one or two victims to the *marae* of 'Oro, where the eyes were scooped out and given to the king ([Haweis] 1798: 111; Turnbull 1813: 381). The encompassing character of sovereignty was not only reflected by this ritual but also tested and created through it, since districts might or might not provide victims. This matter was quite central to political struggles and new configurations which developed in Tahiti around the beginning of the nineteenth century. The issue was essentially whether or not the island as a whole would recognize the authority and legitimacy of the Pomare line, from the Pare–Arue districts. The *marae* of 'Oro was actually in the territory of Atehuru and since the people of that district considered Pomare II a usurper, they would not permit the ceremony of his 'coronation' to take place. It was only after Pomare subdued the Atehuru districts in 1802 that the sacrifices and ceremonies were completed. The intimate connection between the paramount chiefship and sacrifice is illustrated in responses to the *Bounty* mutineers' suggestions that the practice should be abandoned:

we often tryd in vain to dissuade the Chiefs to drop their Barbarous Customs, who always gave for answer, 'If we do there will be no more chiefs'. (Morrison 1935: 207)

It is not surprising, then, that on Rapanui human sacrifice had nothing to do with the *ariki mau* but was rather connected with the god Makemake, who was closely associated with the bird man cult; demands for human victims were expressed by Makemake through a shaman (or *ivi atua*). The situation of sacrifice in the Marquesas is complicated by inconsistencies between accounts, but it seems that certain shamans who had achieved the status of living gods (*atua*) actually became receivers of sacrifices and consumed the victim, or part of the victim, in a trance. When there was no living *atua*, the sacrifice was carried out jointly by other priests, including shamans. Sources usually suggest that most of the body was not eaten but left at the *me'ae* for the god. The large quantities of charred and broken human bone in some archaeological deposits, however, indicate that bodies were at least sometimes cooked and consumed. This is an instance where the archaeological evidence is clear upon a point which is obscure in ethnographic and historical sources.

13. There are hints that the same processes were taking place on Easter Island (Routledge, Ethnology, I: 52; Notes, IV; 41f.).

6 Travellers philosophical and unphilosophical

1. A typical recent manifestation of this consensus can be found in an overview of initiation (La Fontaine 1985). The weakness of Frazer's writings are traced to his sources, who were supposedly typically 'missionaries who regarded [the people they described] either as benighted heathens, children of the devil, or else ... as innocent reminders of a Golden Age' (1985: 21). But as Leach (1961) demonstrated, the principal flaw in Frazer's use of evidence was that he consistently misquoted and distorted sources which were often adequate enough as descriptions in themselves.

2. Such at least was a typical view in the London Missionary Society (LMS). Of course, the approaches of Protestants and Catholics, and of the numerous denominations and orders, were varied.

3. On the significance of 'method' in colonial practice, see Fabian (in press).

4. Such personal prefaces often discuss the mistakes and embarrassments of early days of fieldwork – which amounts to an indirect way of asserting the ethnographer's competence, since such problems are always shown to have been encompassed by subsequent understanding and insight.

5. David Darling, for example, claimed in one place that the 'taboo' system was quite arbitrary, that prohibitions were 'simply as they pleased to make them' but elsewhere endeavoured to specify and systematize the principles which generated *tapu*, such as rank, associations with deities, and suchlike (Darling, 1834–35: 6 May 1836; compare 'Tapu' section in 'Remarks' appended to the journal).

6. This seems to have been written by the LMS luminary and intellectual Greatheed on the basis of William Pasco Crook's observations, and information from Temoteitei, a Marquesan boy who had been brought back to England.

7. The account of the voyage of the *Duff* was also divided in approximately this way, and it was specifically noted that there was a kind of complementarity between the two sorts of discourse: 'a prior perusal of the dissertations [on "the natural and civil state of Otaheite"] will therefore be useful to those of our readers who desire to have in view the circumstances and established customs of the natives, while they peruse the history' (Wilson 1799: vi). Some ambiguity and uncertainty about which was primary is perhaps reflected in the fact that the so-called 'Preliminary discourse' is in some editions at the beginning of the volume and in others at the end.

8. One singular feature of modern research is that it has no purpose apart from collecting information. But (as with census data) this could not be taken to mean that the data is unproblematic, and not grounded in a particular project, or uncomplicated by the difficulties informants would have in talking to e.g. colonial officials. All of these questions relate to the particular issue of how the ethnographer is perceived, which is, of course, variable.

9. 'Race' and 'nation' seem to have been used almost interchangeably at this time, reflecting the compounding of mental and physical characteristics.

10. The classic study is Smith's *European vision and the South Pacific* (1960). See also Dening (1986) on the extraordinarily successful eighteenth-century pantomime, *Omai*, which was based on Tahitian material.

11. Smith (1960); these ideas persist today in popular literature and tourist advertising about the South Seas. Hawaii is presented as the land of *aloha* (love), which, as Sahlins has pointed out (1985a: 3), is generally mistranslated, since the word formerly referred more to affection and compassion for kin than sexual passion.

12. This blurring homogenization of different times would not, of course, be the same as the far more productive exercise of attempting to demonstrate that basic features of Fijian culture persisted over time and were manifested under different circumstances: such an endeavour would attend to, rather than erase, contextual variation over time.

7 Evolution of another sort: regional systems theory and the Pacific

1. This issue is also considered in a recent restatement of the significance of Polynesian evidence for evolutionary analysis (Kirch and Green 1987). They

emphasize that a variety of historical and adaptive processes need to be incorporated into a general evolutionary model, and break clearly from theories which emphasize 'stages' or unilinear processes. Although in its insistence upon the significance of history, this is a substantial advance upon certain other views within anthropology (e.g. Dunnell 1980), the authors' emphases upon mechanisms derived directly from biological evolution, such as selective pressures and adaptation, are problematic: it is not clear whether this is intended simply as a metaphoric way of discussing certain processes, or whether this type of systemic logic is actually being imputed to the systems described. Apparent reliance upon the notion of adaptation is especially problematic, as the dependence of this concept upon a discredited functionalist view of social and ecological systems has been well established. On this point, see particularly Ingold's study of reindeer economies (1980), which exposes both the theoretical limitations of ecological–evolutionary paradigms, and their inability to account for social determination and the crisis-ridden character of the particular systems with which he is concerned. Another difficulty arises from a partial reliance upon the stratified–unstratified continuum in the description and differentiation of the Polynesian systems: Tonga and Hawaii are taken to exhibit 'convergent' evolution, because both developed 'true class stratification' independently (Kirch and Green 1987: 443); this is to ignore completely the fundamentally divergent nature of these systems of social reproduction – in the former case, but not in the latter, external exchange was clearly crucial. The tendency in this particular article, and in 'evolutionary' writing in archaeology generally, has been to overlook altogether or at least diminish the significance of social processes, and instead discuss imputed systemic mechanisms in terms which sound scientific but seem entirely detached from actual events and processes in the histories of the groups considered.

2. A feature of Tongan society which was consistent with Friedman's model of the prestige-goods form was the separation of religious and secular leadership. This is an aspect of the general pattern of 'dualism' emphasized by Friedman, and is found unevenly across the region. In the Fijian polity of Bau, for instance, there was a sacred paramount (the Roko Tui Bau) and a war chief (the Vunivalu). In Tonga there was actually at one time a trial division with two executive rulers, the Tui Ha'atakalaua and the Tui Kanukupolu (although the former title had been discontinued before contact) and the higher ranking, sacred Tui Tonga. The problem for Friedman's argument is that the Tongan oral traditions which describe the establishment of these titles stress their recency in a precise genealogical time-scale (Gifford 1924). It could be argued that the royal history has fabricated the former existence of a unitary chiefship embracing all functions, but such a claim would only become plausible if supported by specific arguments as to why such a charter should be called for. It is also relevant that the titles are peculiar to Tonga, unlike general terms such as *tui* which are widely distributed in western Polynesia and presumably therefore reflect some older and more general complex. This element of the prestige-goods system is thus very likely to be a late development. Moreover, the archaeological evidence for the trade with Fiji and Samoa which channelled the crucial prestige-goods suggests a date of about 1500 for the beginnings of the pattern of interaction observed by Cook and others late in the eighteenth century (e.g. Davidson 1977, 1978; Kirch 1984). The problem is thus simply that a distinctive early contact situation is taken as a model for a prehistory which spans several millennia.

My discussion of Friedman's work is confined to issues of theoretical significance: his paper on the Pacific contains various more specific mis-interpretations or unwarranted speculations which I do not pursue here.

3. The evidence is not, however, clear cut: the early nineteenth-century Tongan view seems to have been that the assassination which triggered off the long series of civil wars was a reaction to the despotic behaviour of the chiefly victim; it is also suggested that warlike habits were learned from the Fijians (Martin 1827, I: 77–80). There is, of course, no reason why either of these things should not have happened at any time earlier, and it does seem very likely that the visits of the explorers did somehow cause the transformation.

8 Histories structured and unstructured

1. In Munn's work we also find the incorporation of a specific kind of time which is not historical: her phenomenological analysis centres upon intersubjective 'spacetime' but says very little about other sorts of temporality (cf. 1986: 1–11).
2. A curious implication of these claims is a radical devaluation of structure, since if the 'vast scheme' could provide a precedent for *any* action, it can have played no effective structuring role at all.
3. This is, of course, a matter of effect rather than necessary logical connection, since there is no theoretical reason why the tenet about change should not be linked with some different theory of the structural causes of larger trans-formations. But this is neither provided for in Sahlins' theory, nor expressed in any of his substantive analyses.

9 The look of events

1. In a discussion of the anthropological 'Enigma', Roy Wagner mentioned in passing that the context of ethnographic fact might be 'viewed as historical accretion or productive "system"' (1986: xiii). Given the history of anthropology, how else might the alternatives be posed? But in another way of writing, 'context' might equally take the form of historical system or productive accretion.

Bibliography

Abbreviations

BPBMB   Bernice P. Bishop Museum Bulletin
JPH   *Journal of Pacific History*
JPS   *Journal of the Polynesian Society*

Abel, C. W. [1902] *Savage life in New Guinea*. London: London Missionary Society
Acar, Sébastian (1893–96) Journal. Typescript, Archives of the Congregation of the Sacred Hearts of Jesus and Mary, Rome
Adams, H. (1947) *Memoirs of the Ari'i Taimaie*. Paris: privately printed
Alexander, Charlotte (1934) *William Patterson Alexander in Kentucky, the Marquesas, Hawaii*. Honolulu: privately printed
Alexander, James (1895) *The islands of the Pacific*. New York: American Tract Society
Anon. (1817) [Review of Mariner's *Tonga Islands*]. *Monthly Review* **83**: 337–59
Anon. (1868) Among the Pacific Islanders [review and extract of E. H. Lamont, *Wild life among the Pacific Islanders* (London 1867)]. *Chamber's Journal*, January 1868: 55–8
Armstrong, William (1838) A sketch of Marquesan character. *Hawaiian Spectator* **1**: 6–16
Asad, T. (ed.) (1973) *Anthropology and the colonial encounter*. London: Ithaca
Augé, Marc (1982) *The anthropological circle: symbol, function, history*. Cambridge: Cambridge University Press
Austin, Diane J. (1979) Symbols and culture: some philosophical assumptions in the work of Clifford Geertz. *Social Analysis* **3**: 45–59
Banks, Joseph [1962] *The Endeavour journal of Joseph Banks, 1768–1771* (ed. J. C. Beaglehole). Sydney: Public Library of New South Wales/Angus & Robertson
Baré, Jean-François (1985) *Le malentendu Pacifique*. Paris: Hachette
    (1987) *Tahiti, les temps et les pouvoirs: pour une anthropologie historique du Tahiti post-européen*. Paris: Office de la Recherche Scientifique et Technique Outre-Mer
Beaglehole, E. and P. Beaglehole (1938) *Ethnology of Pukapuka*. BPBMB 150
Beaglehole, J. C. – see under Cook
Beattie, John (1965) *Understanding an African kingdom: Bunyoro*. New York: Holt, Rinehart & Winston
Beckett, Jeremy (1987) *Torres Strait islanders: custom and colonialism*. Sydney: Cambridge University Press
Beechey, F. W. (1831) *Narrative of a voyage to the Pacific … 1825–8*. London: Colburn
Bellwood, Peter (1978) *Man's conquest of the Pacific*. Sydney: Nelson
Belshaw, C. S. (1964) *Under the ivi tree*. London: Routledge

Bibliography

Bloch, Maurice (ed.) (1975) *Marxist analyses in social anthropology*. London: Malaby
(1986) *From blessing to violence: history and ideology in the circumcision ritual of the Merina of Madagascar*. Cambridge: Cambridge University Press
(1987) [Review of V. Valeri, *Kingship and sacrifice* (qv)]. *Man* (ns) **22**: 218–19
Borofsky, R. (1987) *Making history: Pukapukan and anthropological constructs of knowledge*. Cambridge: Cambridge University Press
Bourdieu, Pierre (1977) *Outline of a theory of practice*. Cambridge: Cambridge University Press
Brewster, A. B. (1922) *The hill tribes of Fiji*. London: Seeley, Service & Co.
Buck, Peter H. (Te Rangi Hiroa) (1932a) *Ethnology of Manihiki and Rakahanga*. BPBMB 99
(1932b) *Ethnology of Tongareva*. BPBMB 92
(1934) *Mangaian society*. BPBMB 122
(1938) *An introduction to Polynesian anthropology*. BPBMB 187
Burrows, E. G. (1936) *Ethnology of Futuna*. BPBMB 138
(1937) *Ethnology of Uvea*. BPBMB 145
(1939) *Western Polynesia: a study in cultural differentiation*. Gothenberg: Ethnological Studies
Campbell, John (1840) *Maritime exploration and Christian missions*. London: John Snow
Chaulet, Pierre (AMS = n.d.) Archipel des Marquises ou de Mendana. Supplément: les Marquises payennes. MS, Archives, Diocese of Taiohae, Nukuhiva, Marquesas Islands
(1873) Notices géographiques, ethnographiques et religieuses sur les îles Marquises. MS, Archives, Congregation of the Sacred Hearts of Jesus and Mary, Rome
Churchward, William (1887) *My consulate in Samoa*. London: Bentley
Claessen, H. and P. Skalnik (1981) *The early state*. The Hague: Mouton
Clifford, James (1986) Introduction: partial truths. In Clifford and Marcus (eds.), *Writing culture* (qv)
(1988) *The predicament of culture*. Cambridge, Mass.: Harvard University Press
Clifford, James and George E. Marcus (eds.) (1986) *Writing culture: the poetics and politics of ethnography*. Berkeley: University of California Press
Clunie, Fergus (1986) *Yalo i Viti. Shades of Fiji: a Fiji Museum catalogue*. Suva: Fiji Museum
Cohn, Bernard S. (1980) History and anthropology: the state of play. *Comparative Studies in Society and History* **22**: 198–221
Cohn, N. (1970) *Pursuit of the millennium: revolutionary millenarianisms and mystical anarchists of the Middle Ages*. New York: Oxford University Press
Comaroff, Jean (1985) *Body of power, spirit of resistance: the culture and history of a South African people*. Chicago: Chicago University Press
Cook, James [1955] *The journals of Captain James Cook on his voyages of discovery. Volume I. The voyage of the Endeavour...* (ed. J. C. Beaglehole). Cambridge: Hakluyt Society
[1961] *The journals... Volume II. The voyage of the Resolution and Adventure, 1772–1775* (ed. J. C. Beaglehole). Cambridge: Hakluyt Society
[1967] *The journals... Volume III. The voyage of the Resolution and Discovery* (ed. J. C. Beaglehole). Cambridge: Hakluyt Society
Crook, William Pascoe (1800) An account of the Marquesas Islands. MS, Mitchell Library, Sydney
Darling, David (1834–35) Journals at Vaitahu [Marquesas]. MS, South Seas Journals, Council for World Mission collection, School of Oriental and African Studies, London

Davenport, William H. (1986) Two kinds of value in the Eastern Solomon Islands. In Arjun Appadurai (ed.), *The social life of things*. Cambridge: Cambridge University Press

Davidson, Janet (1977) Western Polynesia and Fiji: prehistoric contact, diffusion and differentiation in adjacent archipelagoes. *World Archaeology* **9**: 82–94

(1978) Western Polynesia and Fiji: the archaeological evidence. *Mankind* (special issue, *Trade and exchange in Oceania and Australia*, J. Specht and J. P. White (eds.)) **11**: 383–90

Davidson, J. W. (1955 [1966]) Problems of Pacific history. *JPH* **1**: 5–21

Dening, Greg (1980) *Islands and beaches. Discourse on a silent land: Marquesas 1774–1880*. Melbourne: Melbourne University Press

(1986) Possessing Tahiti. *Archaeology in Oceania* **21**: 103–18

Dumont D'Urville, J. S. C. (1832) Sur les îles du Grand Océan. *Société de Géographie Bulletin* **17**: 1–21

Dunnell, R. C. (1980) Evolutionary theory and archaeology. *Advances in Archaeological Method and Theory* **3**: 38–99

Dupetit-Thouars, Abel (1840–43) *Voyage autour du monde ... 1836–39*. Paris: Gide

Eggan, Fred (1949) The Hopi and the lineage principle. In Fortes (ed.), *Social structure* (qv)

Ekholm, Kajsa (1977) External exchange and the transformation of central African social systems. In Friedman and Rowlands (eds.), *The evolution of social systems* (qv)

(1981 [orig. 1976]) On the structure and dynamics of global systems. In Joel S. Kahn and Josep R. Llobera (eds.), *The anthropology of pre-capitalist societies*. London: Macmillan

Elkin, A. P. (1956) A. R. Radcliffe-Brown, 1880–1955 [obituary]. *Oceania* **24**: 239–51

Ellis, William (1829) *Polynesian researches*. London: Fisher & Jackson

(1831) *Polynesian researches*. (4 vol. edn.) Reprint, Rutland, Vermont: Tuttle

Evans-Pritchard, E. E. (1949) *The Sanusi of Cyrenaica*. Oxford: Oxford University Press

(1962) History and anthropology. In Evans-Pritchard, *Essays in social anthropology*. London: Faber & Faber.

(1981) *A history of anthropological thought*. London: Faber & Faber

Fabian, Johannes (1983) *Time and the other: how anthropology makes its object*. New York: Columbia University Press

(1986) *Language and colonial power*. Cambridge: Cambridge University Press

(in press) Religious and secular colonialism: common ground. *History and Anthropology* **4**

Firth, Raymond (1929) *Primitive economics of the New Zealand Maori*. New York: E. P. Dutton

(1936) *We, the Tikopia*. London: Allen & Unwin

Flenley, J. P. (1979) Stratigraphic evidence of environmental change on Easter Island. *Asian Perspectives* **22**: 33–40

Fleurieu, C. P. de C. (1801) *A voyage round the world performed during the years 1790, 1791 & 1792 by Etienne Marchand*. London: Longman Rees

Fornander, A. (1878–80) *An account of the Polynesian race*. Reprint, Rutland, Vermont: Tuttle

Forster, Johann Reinhold (1778) *Observations made during a voyage round the world*. London: Robinson.

[1982] *The Resolution journal of Johann Reinhold Forster* (ed. Michael E. Hoare). London: Hakluyt Society

Fortes, Meyer (1949a) Preface. In Fortes (ed.), *Social structure* (qv)

(1949b) *The web of kinship amongst the Tallensi*. Oxford: Oxford University Press

(ed.) (1949) *Social structure: studies presented to A. R. Radcliffe-Brown*. Oxford: Oxford University Press

Foster, Robert J. (1987) Thick beyond description: ethnography and culture as trope [review article on Roy Wagner's *Asiwinarong* and *Symbols which stand for themselves* (both 1986)]. *Oceania* **58**: 148–56

Fox, J. J. (1977) *Harvest of the palm*. Cambridge, Mass.: Harvard University Press

Frankel, S. (1986) *The Huli response to illness*. Cambridge: Cambridge University Press

Freeman, Derek (1983) *Margaret Mead and Samoa*. Canberra: Australian National University Press

Friedman, Jonathon (1972) Marxism, structuralism and vulgar materialism. *Man* **9**: 444–69

(1981) Notes on structure and history in Oceania. *Folk* **23**: 275–95

(1985) Captain Cook, culture and the world system. *JPH* **20**: 191–201

Friedman J. and M. J. Rowlands (eds.) (1977) *The evolution of social systems*. London: Duckworth

Geertz, Clifford (1968) *Islam observed*. Chicago: Chicago University Press

(1973) *The interpretation of cultures: essays in interpretive anthropology*. New York: Basic Books

(1980) *Negara: the theatre state in nineteenth-century Bali*. Princeton, NJ: Princeton University Press

(1983) *Local knowledge: further essays in interpretive anthropology*. New York: Basic Books

Gewertz, Deborah (1983) *Sepik river societies*. New Haven: Yale University Press

Giddens, Anthony (1979) *Central problems in social theory*. London: Macmillan

(1981) *A contemporary critique of historical materialism*. London: Macmillan

Gifford, E. W. (1924) *Tongan myths and tales*. BPBMB 8

(1929) Tongan society. BPBMB 61

Gill, William Wyatt (1876a) *Life in the southern isles*. London: Religious Tract Society

(1876b) *Myths and songs from the south Pacific*. London: King

(1894) *From darkness to light in Polynesia*. Reprint, Suva: University of the South Pacific

(1916) *Rarotonga records*. New Plymouth, NZ: Polynesian Society

Gilmour, James (1883) *Among the Mongols*. London: Religious Tract Society

Gilson, Richard (1980) *The Cook Islands: 1820–1950*. Wellington: Victoria University Press

Godelier, Maurice (1977) *Perspectives in Marxist anthropology*. Cambridge: Cambridge University Press

Goldman, Irving (1955) Status rivalry and cultural evolution in Polynesia. *American Anthropologist* **57**: 680–97

(1970) *Ancient Polynesian society*. Chicago: Chicago University Press

Golson, Jack (1971) Lapita ware and its transformations. In R. Green and M. Kelly (eds.), *Studies in Oceanic culture history*. Honolulu: BPBM

Goodenough, Ward H. (1957) Oceania and the problem of controls in the study of cultural and human evolution. *JPS* **66**: 146–55

Gunn, William (1914) *The Gospel in Futuna*. London: Hodder & Stoughton

Gunson, Niel (1979) The *hau* concept of leadership in western Polynesia. *JPH* **14**: 28–49

(1982) Polynesian studies: a decade of Tahitian history. *JPH* **17** (Bibliography and Comment supplement): 66–72

Hale, Horatio (1846) *United States exploring expedition. Ethnology and philology.* Philadelphia: Lea & Blanchard

Handy, E. S. C. (1923) *The native culture in the Marquesas.* BPBMB 9

(1930) *History and culture in the Society Islands.* BPBMB 79

Handy, E. S. C. and M. K. Pukui (1958) *The Polynesian family system in Ka'u, Hawaii.* Willington: Polynesian Society

Handy, W. C. (1923) *Tattooing in the Marquesas.* BPBMB 1

(1938) *L'art des îles Marquises.* Paris: Les éditions d'art et d'histoire

(1965) *Forever the land of men.* New York

[Haweis, Thomas] (1798) On the Otaheitian sacrifice. *Evangelical Magazine*, Feb. 1798: 110–12.

Henry, Teuira (1928) *Ancient Tahiti.* BPBMB 48

Hjarno, J. (1979/80) Social reproduction: towards an understanding of aboriginal Samoa. *Folk* **21–22**: 72–123

Hoare, Michael E. (1976) *The tactless philosopher: Johann Reinhold Forster, 1729–98.* Melbourne: Hawthorn Press

Hogbin, H. Ian (1931) The social organization of Ontong Java. *Oceania* **1**: 399–425

Hooper, Antony (1985) Introduction. In A. Hooper and J. Huntsman (eds.) *Transformations of Polynesian culture.* Auckland: Polynesian Society

Hooper, S. J. P. (1982) A study of valuables in the chiefdom of Lau, Fiji. PhD thesis, University of Cambridge

Howard, Alan (1972) Polynesian social stratification revisited: reflections on castles built of sand (and a few bits of coral). *American Anthropologist* **74**: 811–23

Howe, K. R. (1984) *Where the waves fall: a new South Seas history from first settlement to colonial rule.* Sydney: Allen & Unwin

Humphrey, Caroline (1982) *Karl Marx collective.* Cambridge: Cambridge University Press

Im Thurn, E. and L. Wharton (eds.) (1925) *The journal of William Lockerby ... with other papers.* London: Hakluyt Society

Ingold, Tim (1980) *Hunters, pastoralists and ranchers.* Cambridge: Cambridge University Press

(1986) *Evolution and social life.* Cambridge: Cambridge University Press

IWGIA (1987) *International Work Group on Indigenous Affairs. Yearbook 1986.* Copenhagen: IWGIA

Jolly, Margaret (1987) The chimera of equality in Melanesia. *Mankind* (special issue, *Equality and inequality*, I. Bedford, G. Bottomley and A. Hamilton (eds.)) **17**: 168–83

Kaeppler, Adrienne (1978) Exchange patterns in good and spouses: Fiji, Tonga and Samoa. *Mankind* (special issue, *Trade and exchange in Oceania and Australia*, J. Specht and J. P. White (eds.)) **11**: 246–52

Kamakau, S. M. (1964) *Ka Po'e Kahiko: the people of old.* Honolulu: Bishop Museum Press

Keesing, Roger M. (1985) Kwaio women speak: the micropolitics of autobiography in a Solomon Island society. *American Anthropologist* **87**: 27–39

(1987) Anthropology as interpretive quest. *Current Anthropology* **28**: 161–76

Kekela, James (1854) Marquesas, island of Fatuhiva. *The Friend* **11**: 26–7

Kent, Noel J. (1983) *Hawaii: islands under the influence.* New York: Monthly Review.

Kirch, Patrick Vinton (1984) *The evolution of the Polynesian chiefdoms.* Cambridge: Cambridge University Press

(1986) Rethinking east Polynesian prehistory. *JPS* **95**: 9–40

(ed.) (1986) *Island societies: archaeological approaches to evolution and transformation.* Cambridge: Cambridge University Press

Kirch, Patrick Vinton and Roger C. Green (1987) History, phylogeny and evolution in Polynesia. *Current Anthropology* **28**: 431–56

Krusenstern, A. J. von (1813) *Voyage round the world...1803–1806.* London: John Murray

Kuper, Adam (1973) *Anthropologists and anthropology: the British school 1922–1972.* Harmondsworth: Penguin

La Fontaine, J. S. (1985) *Initiation.* Harmondsworth: Penguin

Lakatos, I. and J. Musgrave (1970) *Criticism and the growth of knowledge.* Cambridge: Cambridge University Press

Langham, Ian (1981) *The building of British social anthropology.* Dordrecht: Reidel

La Pérouse, J. F. G. de (1797) *Voyage autour du monde...* Paris

Latukefu, Sione (1970) King George Tupou I of Tonga. In J. W. Davidson and Deryck Scarr (eds.), *Pacific islands portraits.* Canberra: Australian National University Press

Lawson, Thomas (1868) Letter to Gulick, MS in Marquesas collection, Hawaiian Mission Children's Society Library, Honolulu

Leach, Edmund (1954) *Political systems of highland Burma.* London: Athlone

(1961) Golden bough or gilded twig? *Daedalus*, Spring 1961: 371–86

(1973) *Custom, law and terrorist violence.* Edinburgh: Edinburgh University Press

Leacock, Eleanor and Richard Lee (1982) *Politics and history in band societies.* Cambridge: Cambridge University Press

Lederman, R. (1986) *What gifts engender.* Cambridge: Cambridge University Press

Leenhardt, Maurice (1947) *Do kamo: la personne et la mythe dans le monde mélanesien.* Paris: Institut d'Ethnologie

Lévi-Strauss, Claude (1966) *The savage mind.* London: Weidenfeld & Nicolson

(1968) Introduction: History and anthropology, in *Structural anthropology.* Harmondsworth: Penguin

Lewis, I. M. (ed.) (1968) *History and social anthropology.* London: Tavistock Publications

(1986) *Religion in context: cults and charisma.* Cambridge: Cambridge University Press

Linnekin, Jocelyn (1984) *Children of the land: exchange and status in a Hawaiian community.* New Brunswick: Rutgers University Press

Linton, Ralph (1923) *The material culture of the Marquesas Islands.* BPBM Memoir 8, Part 5.

(1925) *Archaeology of the Marquesas Islands.* BPBMB 23

(1939) Marquesan culture. In Abram Kardiner, *The individual and his society.* New York: Columbia University Press

Lisiansky, U. (1814) *A voyage round the world...1803–1806.* London: John Booth

Loeb, E. M. (1926) *History and traditions of Niue.* BPBMB 32

Macgregor, Gordon (1937) *Ethnology of Tokelau.* BPBMB 146

Macnaught, Timothy J. (1982) *The Fijian colonial experience.* Canberra: Research School of Pacific Studies, Australian National University

Malinowski, Bronislaw (1922) *Argonauts of the western Pacific.* London: Routledge

Malo, D. (1951) *Hawaiian antiquities.* Honolulu: Bernice P. Bishop Museum Special Publication

Marcus, George E. and Michael J. J. Fischer (1986) *Anthropology as cultural critique.* Chicago: Chicago University Press

148

Martin, John (1827) *An account of the natives of the Tonga Islands in the South Pacific Ocean...from the extensive communications of Mr. William Mariner...* (3rd edn.). Edinburgh: Constable

Marzan, Jean de (1908) Sur quelques sociétés secrètes aux îles Fiji. *Anthropos* **3**: 718–28

Maude, H. E. (1968) *Of islands and men.* Melbourne: Oxford University Press

(1982) *Slavers in paradise: the Peruvian labour trade in Polynesia, 1862–63.* Canberra: Australian National University Press

McCoy, P. (1979) Easter Island. In Jesse D. Jennings (ed.), *The Prehistory of Polynesia.* Canberra: Australian National University Press

Mead, Margaret (1930) *The social organization of Manua.* BPBMB 76

Métraux, Alfred (1940) *Ethnology of Easter Island.* BPBMB 160

Moore, S. F. (1986) *Social facts and fabrications: 'customary' law on Kilimanjaro, 1880–1980.* Cambridge: Cambridge University Press

Moorehead, Alan (1968) *The fatal impact.* Harmondsworth: Penguin

Morrison, James [1935] *The journal of James Morrison...together with an account of the island of Tahiti* (ed. O. Rutter). London: Golden Cockerel Press

Morton-Williams, P. (1968) The Fulani penetration into Nupe and Yoruba in nineteenth century. In Lewis (ed.), *History and social anthropology* (qv)

Mouat, F. J. (1863) *Adventures and researches among the Andaman Islanders.* London

Munn, Nancy (1986) *The fame of Gawa.* Cambridge: Cambridge University Press

Nayacakalou, R. (1975) *Leadership in Fiji.* Melbourne: Oxford University Press

Needham, Rodney (1974) *Remarks and inventions: sceptical essays about kinship.* London: Chicago University Press

Oliver, Douglas L. (1974) *Ancient Tahitian society.* Canberra: Australian National University Press

Ollivier, Pacôme (1867) Lettre du...[concerning Easter Island]. *Annales de la propagation de la foi* **39**: 250–9

Ortner, Sherry B. (1981) Gender and sexuality in hierarchical societies: the case of Polynesia and some comparative implications. In Sherry B. Ortner and Harriet Whitehead (eds.), *Sexual meanings: the cultural construction of gender and sexuality.* Cambridge: Cambridge University Press

Palmer, J. Linton (1870) A visit to Easter Island or Rapa Nui in 1868. *Journal of the Royal Geographical Society* **40**: 167–81

Parmentier, R. J. (1987) *The sacred remains: myth, history and polity in Belau.* Chicago: Chicago University Press

Pawley, Andrew (1981) Melanesian diversity and Polynesian homogeneity: a unified explanation for language. In A. Pawley and J. Hollyman (eds.), *Studies in Pacific languages and cultures in honour of Bruce Biggs.* Auckland: Linguistic Society of New Zealand

Portman, M. V. (1899) *A history of our relations with the Andamanese.* Calcutta: Govt. Printer

Radcliffe-Brown [then Brown], A. R. (1922) *The Andaman Islanders.* Cambridge: Cambridge University Press

(1931) *The social organization of Australian tribes.* Sydney: Oceania Monographs

Ralston, Caroline (1988) Ordinary women in early post-contact Hawaii. In M. Jolly and M. Macintyre (eds.), *Family and gender in the Pacific: domestic contradictions and the colonial impact.* Cambridge: Cambridge University Press

Robarts, Edward [1974] *The Marquesan journal of Edward Robarts* (ed. G. Dening). Canberra: Australian National University Press

Roggeveen, Jacob (1722 [1908]) *Extracts from the official log of Mynheer J. Roggeveen*

(1721–22) ...in Don Felipe Gonzalez y Haedo, The voyage to Easter Island in 1770–1771 (ed. B. Corney). London: Hakluyt Society

Rosaldo, R. (1980) *Ilongot headhunting, 1883–1974*. Stanford: Stanford University Press

Routledge, Katherine Scoresby (1917) The bird cult of Easter Island. *Folklore* **28**: 337–55

(n.d.) Ethnology (vols. 1–2). MS, Royal Geographical Society

(n.d.) Notes [on Easter Island] (vols. 3–4). MS, Royal Geographical Society

Rutherford, Noel (1977) *Friendly Islands: a history of Tonga*. Melbourne: Oxford University Press

Ryazanov, N. P. (1825) [The first voyage of the Russians around the world]. *Otechestvennye Zapiski* **24**: 73–96; 386–96 (in Russian)

Sagan, Eli (1985) *At the dawn of tyranny*. London: Faber & Faber

Sahlins, Marshall (1958) *Social stratification in Polynesia*. Seattle: American Ethnological Society

(1962) *Moala: culture and nature on a Fijian island*. Ann Arbor: University of Michigan Press

(1981) *Historical metaphors and mythical realities: structure in the early history of the Sandwich Island kingdom*. Ann Arbor: University of Michigan Press

(1985a) *Islands of history*. Chicago: Chicago University Press

(1985b) Hierarchy and humanity in Polynesia. In A. Hooper and J. Huntsman (eds.), *Transformations of Polynesian culture*. Auckland: Polynesian Society

Ste. Croix, G. E. M. de (1981) *The class struggle in the ancient Greek world*. London: Duckworth

Seabrook, A. (n.d.) Rurutuan culture. MS, Bishop Museum

Seddon, D. (ed.) (1978) *Relations of production*. London: F. Cass

Service, E. R. (1975) *Origins of the state and civilization*. New York: Norton

Shillibeer, J. (1817) *A narrative of the Briton's voyage to Pitcairn's Island*. Taunton: Marriot

Shore, B. (1982) *Sala'ilua: a Samoan mystery*. New York: Columbia University Press

Slayter, Thomas (1843) May meeting in the Samoas. *Missionary magazine and chronicle* **7**: 54

Smith, Bernard (1960) *European vision and the South Pacific*. Oxford: Oxford University Press

Spriggs, M. J. T. (1981) Vegetable kingdoms: taro irrigation and Pacific prehistory. PhD thesis, Australian National University

Stair, John B. (1897) *Old Samoa*. London: Religious Tract Society

Stevenson, Robert Louis (1900) *In the South Seas*. London: Chatto & Windus

Steward, J. (1955) *Theory of culture change*. Urbana: University of Illinois Press

Stocking, George W. (1968) *Race, language and culture*. New York: Free Press

(1984) Radcliffe-Brown and British social anthropology. In Stocking (ed.), *Functionalism historicized: essays on British social anthropology* (History of Anthropology, vol. 2). Madison: University of Wisconsin Press

(ed.) (1985) *Objects and others: essays on museums and material culture*. (History of anthropology, vol. 3). Madison: University of Wisconsin Press

Stokes, J. F. (n.d.) Ethnology of Rapa. MS, Bishop Museum

Tambiah, S. J. (1970) *Buddhism and the spirit cults in north-east Thailand*. Cambridge: Cambridge University Press

Thomas, Keith (1971) *Religion and the decline of magic*. Harmondsworth: Penguin

Thomas, Nicholas (1985) Forms of personification and prestations. *Mankind* **15**: 223–30

(1986a) '*Le roi de Tahuata*': Iotete and the transformation of south Marquesan politics, 1826–1842. *JPH* **21**: 3–20

(1986b) Gender and social relations in Polynesia: a critical note. *Canberra Anthropology* **9**: 78–89

(1987) Complementarity and history: misrecognizing gender in the Pacific. *Oceania* **57**: 259–70

(1990) *Marquesan societies: inequality and political transformations in eastern Oceania*. Oxford: Oxford University Press

(n.d.1) Politicized values: barter and exchange on colonial peripheries. In Caroline Humphrey and Stephen Hugh-Jones (eds.), *Barter, exchange and value*. Cambridge: Cambridge University Press

(n.d.2) Substantivization in anthropological discourse: the transformation of practices into institutions in neotraditional Pacific societies. In James W. Carrier (ed.), *Tradition, history and articulation in Melanesian anthropology*, forthcoming

Thompson, E. P. (1963) *The making of the English working class*. Harmondsworth: Penguin

Thompson, Laura (1940) *Southern Lau: an ethnography*. BPBMB 162

Thomson, Basil (1908) *The Fijians: a study in the decay of custom*. London: Macmillan

Thomson, W. J. (1889) *Te Pito te Henua or Easter Island*. In US National Museum Annual Report: 447–552

Tjibao, J.-M. and P. H. Missotte (trans. C. Plant) (1978) *Kanaké: the Melanesian way*. Papeete, Tahiti: Les editions du pacifique

Troost, C. P. (1829) *Aanteekeningen gehouden op eene reis om dem wereld...1824–26*. Rotterdam

Turnbull, John (1813) *A voyage around the world...1800–1804* (2nd edn.). London: A. Maxwell

Turner, George (1884) *Samoa a hundred years ago and long before*. London: J. Snow

Urry, James (1983) [Review of Langham, *The Building of British social anthropology* (qv)]. *Oceania* **53**: 400–2

Valeri, Valerio (1985) *Kingship and sacrifice: ritual and society in ancient Hawaii*. Chicago: Chicago University Press

Wagner, Roy (1986) *Asiwinarong: ethos, image and social power among the Usen Barok of New Ireland*. Princeton: Princeton University Press

White, Caroline (1981) *Patrons and partisans: a study of two southern Italian comuni*. Cambridge: Cambridge University Press

White, Isobel (1981) Mrs Bates and Mr Brown: an examination of Rodney Needham's allegations. *Oceania* **51**: 193–210

Whittaker, Ian (1968) Tribal structure and national politics in Albania, 1910–1950. In Lewis (ed.), *History and social anthropology* (qv)

Williams, Thomas (1884 [orig. 1858]) *Fiji and the Fijians*. London: T. Woolmer

[1931] *The journal of Thomas Williams, Fiji 1840–1853* (ed. G. C. Henderson). Sydney: Angus & Robertson

Williamson, R. W. (1924) *The social and political systems of central Polynesia*. Cambridge: Cambridge University Press

Wilson, William [*et al.*] (1799) *A missionary voyage in the southern Pacific Ocean...1796–1798*. London: T. Chapman

Wood, Michael (1982) Kamula social structure and ritual. PhD thesis, Macquarie University

Worsley, Peter (1957) *The trumpet shall sound: a study of 'cargo' cults in Melanesia.* London: MacGibbon and Kee

Young, Michael W. (1983) *Magicians of Manumanua: living myth in Kalauna.* Berkeley: California University Press.

Index

Abel, C. W., 70–71
agency, in colonial history, 111–14
Andaman Islanders, 21–23, 26, 55, 119, 125 n6
Aneityum, 53
anthropology, history of, 19
anthropology, professionalization of, 19–20, 22–24, 125 n8
anthropology, symbolic, 7–8, 9, 16
archaeology, 66, 115, 122, 124 n5
Augé, M., 125 n5
Australian Aborigines, 23–24, 106, 107, 125 n7

Bali, 26, 126 n9
Barolong, 7
Bates, D., 125, n7
Beattie, J., 13
Belshaw, C. S., 83
Benedict, R., 18
Bishop Museum, 18, 32, 42, 43–49, 128 n5, 129 n6, n8, n9
Boas, F., 18, 33
Borofsky, R., 129 n5
Boswell, J., 75
Bougainville, L. de, 42, 54, 78
Bourdieu, P., 5, 102, 108
Buck, P., 32, 44–48, 129, n6
Bunyoro, 13
Burrows, E. W., 45

Campbell, J., 31, 32
Chagga, 7
Chaulet, P., 64, 74–75, 83, 130 n2, 132 n9
chieftainship, 29, 40, 52–53, 55, 56–58, 60–61, 104–5, 132 nn 9, 12
Churchward, W., 32
Clunie, F., 82

Cohn, B., 3, 11
colonial history, 10, 17, 55–56, 82, 96–101, 111, 116, 123 n1
Comaroff, J., 7
Cook, Capt. J., 29, 42, 62, 75, 77, 78, 103–6, 107
Cook Islands, 128 n2
Crook, W., 74, 134 n6
cultural materialism, 9

Darling, D., 134 n5
Delmas, S., 52
Dening, G., 134 n9
detective stories, 118–19
'devolution', 65
Dumont D'Urville, J. S. C., 31

Easter Island, see Rapanui
ecological change, 61–64
Ekholm, K., 16, 87–89, 97
Elkin, A. P., 125 n7
Ellis, W., 57, 71
epistemological models, 2, 7, 12–14, 17, 33–34, 49–50, 67–68, 119–20
ethnohistory, 3, 125 n5
Evans-Pritchard, 6, 18, 21, 123 n2
events, interpretation of, 80–85, 108–9, 117–19
evolution, concepts of, 3–4, 36–41, 49–50, 86–101, 121–22, 134–35 n1
evolutionism, covert, 17, 28, 35, 109–11, 114, 121–22, 127 n2

Fabian, J., 118, 119
feminist critique, 48
fieldwork, status of, 13, 25, 70, 74, 79, 84–85, 122
Fiji, 79, 80, 82–83, 91, 100, 135 n2, 136 n3

153

Ann Arbor Paperbacks

Waddell, *The Desert Fathers*
Erasmus, *The Praise of Folly*
Donne, *Devotions*
Malthus, *Population: The First Essay*
Berdyaev, *The Origin of Russian Communism*
Einhard, *The Life of Charlemagne*
Edwards, *The Nature of True Virtue*
Gilson, *Héloïse and Abélard*
Aristotle, *Metaphysics*
Kant, *Education*
Boulding, *The Image*
Duckett, *The Gateway to the Middle Ages* (3 vols.): *Italy; France and Britain; Monasticism*
Bowditch and Ramsland, *Voices of the Industrial Revolution*
Luxemburg, *The Russian Revolution and Leninism or Marxism?*
Rexroth, *Poems from the Greek Anthology*
Zoshchenko, *Scenes from the Bathhouse*
Thrupp, *The Merchant Class of Medieval London*
Procopius, *Secret History*
Adcock, *Roman Political Ideas and Practice*
Swanson, *The Birth of the Gods*
Xenophon, *The March Up Country*
Trotsky, *The New Course*
Buchanan and Tullock, *The Calculus of Consent*
Hobson, *Imperialism*
Pobedonostsev, *Reflections of a Russian Statesman*
Kinietz, *The Indians of the Western Great Lakes 1615–1760*
Bromage, *Writing for Business*
Lurie, *Mountain Wolf Woman, Sister of Crashing Thunder*
Leonard, *Baroque Times in Old Mexico*
Meier, *Negro Thought in America, 1880–1915*
Burke, *The Philosophy of Edmund Burke*
Michelet, *Joan of Arc*
Conze, *Buddhist Thought in India*
Arberry, *Aspects of Islamic Civilization*
Chesnutt, *The Wife of His Youth and Other Stories*
Gross, *Sound and Form in Modern Poetry*
Zola, *The Masterpiece*
Chesnutt, *The Marrow of Tradition*
Aristophanes, *Four Comedies*
Aristophanes, *Three Comedies*

Chesnutt, *The Conjure Woman*
Duckett, *Carolingian Portraits*
Rapoport and Chammah, *Prisoner's Dilemma*
Aristotle, *Poetics*
Peattie, *The View from the Barrio*
Duckett, *Death and Life in the Tenth Century*
Langford, *Galileo, Science and the Church*
McNaughton, *The Taoist Vision*
Anderson, *Matthew Arnold and the Classical Tradition*
Milio, *9226 Kercheval*
Weisheipl, *The Development of Physical Theory in the Middle Ages*
Breton, *Manifestoes of Surrealism*
Gershman, *The Surrealist Revolution in France*
Lester, *Theravada Buddhism in Southeast Asia*
Scholz, *Carolingian Chronicles*
Marković, *From Affluence to Praxis*
Wik, *Henry Ford and Grass-roots America*
Sahlins and Service, *Evolution and Culture*
Wickham, *Early Medieval Italy*
Waddell, *The Wandering Scholars*
Rosenberg, *Bolshevik Visions* (2 parts in 2 vols.)
Mannoni, *Prospero and Caliban*
Aron, *Democracy and Totalitarianism*
Shy, *A People Numerous and Armed*
Taylor, *Roman Voting Assemblies*
Goodfield, *An Imagined World*
Hesiod, *The Works and Days; Theogony; The Shield of Herakles*
Raverat, *Period Piece*
Lamming, *In the Castle of My Skin*
Fisher, *The Conjure-Man Dies*
Strayer, *The Albigensian Crusades*
Lamming, *The Pleasures of Exile*
Lamming, *Natives of My Person*
Glaspell, *Lifted Masks and Other Works*
Wolff, *Aesthetics and the Sociology of Art*
Grand, *The Heavenly Twins*
Cornford, *The Origin of Attic Comedy*
Allen, *Wolves of Minong*
Brathwaite, *Roots*
Fisher, *The Walls of Jericho*
Lamming, *The Emigrants*
Loudon, *The Mummy!*
Kemble and Butler Leigh, *Principles and Privilege*
Thomas, *Out of Time*